Love to God
by Thomas Tuke
with chapters by C. Matthew McMahon

Copyright Information

Love to God, by Thomas Tuke
with chapters by C. Matthew McMahon
Edited by Therese B. McMahon

Copyright ©2025 by Puritan Publications and A Puritan's Mind™

Some language and grammar has been updated from the original manuscript. Any change in wording or punctuation has not changed the intent or meaning of the original author(s), and has been made to aid the modern reader.

Published by Puritan Publications
A Ministry of A Puritan's Mind™ in Crossville, TN.
www.apuritansmind.com
www.puritanpublications.com

All rights reserved. No part of this publication may be reproduced, stored in a retrieval system or transmitted in any form by any means, electronic, mechanical, photocopy, recording or otherwise, without the prior permission of the publisher, except as provided by USA copyright law.

This Print Edition, 2025
Electronic Edition, 2025
Manufactured in the United States of America

ISBN: 978-1-62663-515-9
eISBN: 978-1-62663-514-2

Table of Contents

The Mirror of the Soul 4

Meet Thomas Tuke 21

Themes of the Work 26

Introductory Letter 29

PART 1: Exploring Psalm 31 34

PART 2: The Object of Love 40

PART 3: The Excellence of Love 51

PART 4: What Do You Love? 66

PART 5: God Loved in His Church 73

PART 6: God Loved in His Son 78

Other Works Published by Puritan Publications 95

The Mirror of the Soul
By C. Matthew McMahon, Ph.D., Th.D.

Thomas Tuke begins this work with a powerful exhortation rooted in Psalm 31:23: "Love ye the LORD, all his saints: for the LORD preserveth the faithful, and plentifully rewardeth the proud doer," (Psalm 31:23). This verse functions as both an anchor and a lens for the entire treatise, setting the stage for Tuke's theological framework and pastoral urgency. Tuke uses this Scripture to emphasize the heart of Christian life—love for the Lord. For Tuke, this love is no sentimental or superficial affection but the deepest devotion of the soul to its Creator. The imagery of a "looking-glass" in the title aptly captures his purpose: to provide a tool for self-examination that reflects not just the flaws and blemishes of the human condition but also the glory and holiness of God as the standard for Christian living.

The concept of a *mirror* is central to Tuke's intent. A mirror does not distort but reveals, exposing what is real even when the truth is uncomfortable. In the same way, Tuke calls his readers to examine their lives under the unflinching clarity of God's Word. This is not an abstract theological *preface*; it is an instant call to action. Tuke invites his readers to confront their spiritual state honestly, asking whether their lives align with the exhortation to love the Lord wholeheartedly. For Tuke, *Scripture* is the ultimate looking-glass, and

Psalm 31:23 serves as the first reflection, revealing the essential Christian duty of love and the consequences of neglecting it.

Tuke's choice of Psalm 31:23 underscores his theological priorities. By beginning with this verse, he roots his discourse in the dual themes of divine grace and Christian responsibility. Many think that sanctification is something God does without the concurrence of the Christian. The command to "love the LORD" is both universal and specific, addressed to "all his saints" and requires Christians to take up what God has given them in his ordinances and use them for all life and godliness. Tuke's focus here is *typically* Reformed: the saints are those sanctified by God's grace, set apart for His purposes, by *their* works and use of God's means. This love is not self-generated; it flows from God's love for His people. As 1 John 4:19 states, "We love him, because he first loved us." The initiative lies with God, but the response is *demanded of man*. Tuke views this dynamic as the essence of the Christian life—a reciprocal relationship where God's grace compels the believer to respond with love and obedience.

This love is more than an emotional response; it is a comprehensive commitment. Tuke makes it clear that loving the Lord requires, the full devotion of the heart, soul, and mind. He challenges his readers to ask whether their affections are truly centered on God or divided by the allure of worldly pursuits. In this sense, the mirror becomes a tool of conviction, reflecting not only what is but also what ought to be. Tuke's pastoral tone is evident here—he does not present this reflection as a means of despair but as an opportunity for transformation. The mirror reveals flaws, but it also points the way to holiness through God's grace.

Tuke's metaphor of the *looking-glass* (a *mirror*) is deeply intertwined with his view of Scripture. For him, the Bible is the ultimate standard of truth, capable of revealing both the nature of God and the state of the human heart. Psalm 31:23, with its dual emphasis on God's preservation of the faithful and His judgment of the proud, exemplifies this dual role. The Word of God is both a comfort *and* a challenge, offering assurance to those who walk in faithfulness while warning those who persist in pride. Tuke's use of this verse as his foundation demonstrates his conviction that Scripture is not merely a book to be read but a mirror to be looked into, studied, and applied.

The reflective nature of Scripture is central to Tuke's theological approach. He views the Bible as more than a text; it is a dynamic tool that exposes sin, reveals grace, and shapes the believer's life. In Psalm 31:23, the faithful are preserved by God's grace, a truth that offers immense comfort to believers. However, this preservation is not passive; it demands active love and obedience. Similarly, the warning to the proud reminds the reader that God's justice is unyielding. The mirror shows both the beauty of God's holiness and the blemishes of human sinfulness, calling the believer to align their life with God's truth.

Tuke's opening establishes self-examination as a fundamental Christian practice. The mirror is not meant to flatter but to confront. Tuke challenges his readers to reflect on their own spiritual condition, in light of the command to love the Lord. This process is deeply personal yet universally applicable, as every believer is called to examine their heart and life. Tuke's use of Psalm 31:23 emphasizes that this self-examination is not optional; it is an essential part of Christian discipleship. The mirror reveals not only the individual's failures but also the immense grace of God, who preserves the faithful and invites the proud to repentance.

For Tuke, self-examination is not, an end in itself but a means to a greater end: *transformation* in love to Christ. The purpose of the mirror is to spur the believer toward greater holiness, deeper love for God, and more faithful obedience to His commands. This sanctifying process is not accomplished through *human effort alone* but through the grace of God, who works *in* the believer to will and to do His good pleasure (Philippians 2:13). Tuke's pastoral concern is evident as he urges his readers to engage with this process earnestly, trusting in God's ability to change hearts and lives.

Loving the Lord: The Foundation of Christian Duty

Tuke begins his discourse with a central command from Psalm 31:23: "Love ye the LORD, all his saints." This divine imperative stands as the *cornerstone* of his theological framework. To Tuke, loving God is not merely an emotional inclination or an abstract idea—it is the very *foundation* of Christian duty. He frames this love as a binding obligation upon all who are sanctified by God's grace, emphasizing that true Christian living springs forth from a heart wholly devoted to the Savior. For Tuke, the exhortation to love God is both *universal* and deeply *personal.* Addressed to "all his saints," the command encompasses the entire community of believers while also demanding an individual response. This duality highlights the corporate and private dimensions of faith, where the believer's love for God manifests not only in solitary devotion but also in shared worship and mutual edification. By directing this command to the saints, Tuke implicitly reminds the reader of their identity as those set apart by God's mercy, urging them to live in a manner befitting their calling.

The Nature of Loving the Lord

Tuke paints a vivid picture of what it means to love God. It is not a fleeting emotion or a mere intellectual assent; it is an act of the will, a decision to prioritize God above all else. This love is holistic, encompassing the entirety of one's being—heart, soul, mind, and strength. Drawing from the greatest commandment in Scripture, "Thou shalt love the Lord thy God with all thy heart, and with all thy soul, and with all thy mind," (Matthew 22:37), Tuke underscores the totality of the devotion required.

This love, Tuke argues, is not self-generated but a response to God's prior love for His people. Quoting 1 John 4:19, "We love him, because he first loved us," Tuke reminds his readers that their ability to love God is grounded in God's initiating grace. This grace transforms the sinner's heart, enabling them to love God rightly. Tuke's theology is unmistakably Reformed here: love for God is not an inherent human capacity but a divine gift, bestowed through the regenerating work of the Holy Spirit.

The Obstacles to Loving God

Tuke does not shy away from addressing the barriers that hinder believers from loving God as they ought. Chief among these, is the human propensity to idolize created things. Wealth, honor, beauty, and worldly pleasures—all these, Tuke warns, can seduce the heart and draw it away from God. He is adamant that the Christian must guard against divided affections, for as Christ declared, "No man can serve two masters,"

(Matthew 6:24). Tuke portrays love for God as exclusive; it tolerates no rivals.

Moreover, Tuke exposes the subtle ways pride undermines love for God. Pride, which ascribes to man what rightly belongs to God, blinds the soul to its dependence on divine grace. It fosters self-sufficiency, leaving little room for genuine devotion. To love God, Tuke insists, is to humble oneself, acknowledging God as the source of every blessing. The believer who fails to do this, risks falling into the very pride that God resists, as the Scripture declares: "God resisteth the proud, but giveth grace unto the humble," (James 4:6).

The Expression of Love for God

Tuke is careful to define how love for God is expressed. It is not a mere profession of words, but a lived reality demonstrated through obedience. Citing Christ's own words, "If ye love me, keep my commandments," (John 14:15), Tuke ties love directly to action. True love for God is visible in the believer's willingness to submit to His will, even when it conflicts with personal desires or societal expectations.

Obedience, however, is not burdensome for the one who truly loves God. Tuke describes it as a joyful act, born out of gratitude rather than obligation. The believer, recognizing the depth of God's love and faithfulness, responds with willing and cheerful compliance. This obedience is not limited to outward actions but includes the internal posture of the heart, where every thought and intention is aligned with God's purposes.

Love as the Basis of All Virtue

Tuke elevates love for God as the root of all Christian virtues. Without love, faith is hollow, and good works are void of meaning. As Paul writes, "Though I bestow all my goods to feed the poor, and though I give my body to be burned, and have not charity, it profiteth me nothing," (1 Corinthians 13:3). Tuke echoes this sentiment, arguing that love for God is the animating principle of the Christian life. It is the wellspring from which flows every act of worship, every deed of kindness, and every moment of perseverance in faith. Without it, the Christian is as lifeless as a branch severed from the vine.

In calling believers to love the Lord, Tuke not only lays the foundation for Christian duty but also provides the key to living a life that reflects the glory of God. By loving God, the believer fulfills the highest purpose of their existence and aligns themselves with the very heart of divine grace.

The Saints: A Community Set Apart

Tuke's exhortation to "all his saints" in Psalm 31:23 calls attention to the distinct and sacred identity of God's people. For Tuke, the term "saints" does not merely denote moral excellence or piety; it signifies those who are set apart by God's sovereign grace, sanctified for His purposes, and bound together in a holy fellowship. The saints are not defined by their own merits but by their relationship to God, who has chosen and consecrated them as His own. This Reformed understanding of sanctification underscores that the Christian community exists not by human effort but by divine initiative.

Tuke emphasizes that being a saint is both a privilege and a responsibility. Saints are the recipients of God's mercy and love, called out of darkness into His marvelous light (1 Peter 2:9). This calling is not an individualistic endeavor; it is inherently communal. To be a saint is to belong to a people who share in the covenant blessings of God, united by their common faith and commitment to His glory. Tuke draws heavily on the biblical image of the church as the body of Christ, where each member contributes to the whole, fostering mutual edification and spiritual growth.

Moreover, Tuke challenges the saints to live lives that reflect their holy calling. Their sanctification must not remain a *theological abstraction* but manifest in *tangible* expressions of love, humility, and obedience. Saints, he argues, are called to be *examples* of *godliness* in a world that often rejects divine truth, even *amidst a church that often rejects God's truth*. As "a city that is set on a hill cannot be hid," (Matthew 5:14), so too must the saints shine as beacons of light in a darkened world, bearing witness to God's transformative power.

In Tuke's view, the community of saints stands as both a testimony to God's grace and a foretaste of the eternal fellowship believers will share with Him. Their lives are to be marked by devotion to God and service to one another, embodying the unity and holiness that reflect the character of their divine Savior.

The Preservation of the Faithful: God's Covenant Care in Christ

Tuke's emphasis on God's preservation of the faithful, drawn from the promise in Psalm 31:23—"the LORD preserveth the faithful"—captures the heart of Reformed theology: the steadfast care of a covenant-keeping God. For Tuke, this preservation is not merely a passive safeguarding; it is an active, divine engagement with those who trust in Him. Faithfulness, in Tuke's understanding, is both a marker of God's grace and a response to it, as the believer's faith is sustained and strengthened by God's unwavering hand.

Central to Tuke's argument is the concept of God's covenantal nature. The preservation of the faithful is rooted in God's promises, a reflection of His immutable character, and seen in the performance of the covenant on Christ's work. Tuke underscores that God does not abandon His people, for His faithfulness is not contingent upon human merit but rests upon His eternal decree. This is a God who engraves His people on the palms of His hands (Isaiah 49:16) and who, through the work of Christ, ensures that no one can pluck them from His grasp (John 10:28). Such preservation, Tuke asserts, is the outworking of divine love and justice, a guarantee that God will complete the good work He has begun in His people (Philippians 1:6).

While Tuke celebrates God's faithfulness, he also highlights the reciprocal nature of this relationship. The faithful are not passive recipients but *active* participants in their sanctification. Preservation involves perseverance, as believers are called to hold fast to the truth, obey God's commands, and live out their faith amidst trials and temptations. Yet even this perseverance is enabled by God's grace, as He equips His people to endure and remain steadfast. Tuke points to examples such as Noah, Daniel, and the apostles, who trusted in God's preserving power even when faced with overwhelming odds.

Moreover, Tuke connects God's *preservation* to the community of faith. The saints are not preserved in isolation; they are kept within the body of Christ, where mutual support and edification strengthen their resolve. This communal aspect underscores the importance of the church as a means of grace, where the faithful are nourished by the Word, sacrament, and fellowship.

In Tuke's theological framework, the preservation of the faithful is both a divine promise and a practical assurance. It provides a bedrock of hope for believers, reminding them that their security rests not in their own strength but in the unchanging character of God. This covenant care compels the Christian to live with confidence, gratitude, and devotion, knowing that they are held in the hands of a faithful Savior.

The Prideful Rebuked: Divine Justice Revealed

Tuke's treatment of the prideful, grounded in the phrase "plentifully rewardeth the proud doer," (Psalm 31:23), is a sobering exploration of divine justice. For Tuke, pride is not merely a personal failing but a root of *rebellion* against God, a sin that distorts the very order of creation. Pride exalts the self in defiance of God's sovereignty, and Tuke spares no words in outlining the folly and consequences of such arrogance.

At its core, pride is a denial of the Creator's rightful place. Tuke points to pride as the sin that led to the downfall of Lucifer, the ruin of Adam and Eve, and the confusion of the builders at Babel. These biblical examples serve as vivid warnings that pride is not a harmless flaw but a destructive force that invites God's judgment. "God resisteth the proud," Tuke reminds his readers, drawing from James 4:6, and the resistance of an almighty God is an insurmountable opposition.

The "reward" for the proud, Tuke explains, is neither accidental nor arbitrary. It is the inevitable outworking of divine justice. God's recompense is "plentiful," not in the sense of abundant blessing but in the fullness of deserved punishment. The prideful are brought low, as demonstrated in the fates of Pharaoh, Nebuchadnezzar, and Herod Agrippa, each humbled by God in ways that reveal His supreme authority. For Tuke, these historical examples are not only judgments but also lessons for the living, urging repentance, before pride leads to ruin.

Tuke's analysis of pride serves as both a warning and a call to humility. Divine justice, he argues, is inseparable from God's holiness. To despise God's rightful place through pride is to court destruction, but to humble oneself is to find grace and restoration in the Lord.

Practical Application: Living Out Love and Humility

Tuke's emphasis on the practical outworking of faith shines in his exploration of Christian *living*, where love and humility are not abstract ideals but tangible expressions of *experimental piety*. This term, rich in the Reformed tradition, refers to the believer's *lived experience* of God's grace—a theology not merely understood in the mind but felt in the soul and evident in daily life. For Tuke, the Christian faith is meant to transform, not merely inform, and this transformation finds its fullest expression in a life devoted to God and others.

To *love the Lord* is the primary command, the root from which all Christian virtues grow. Tuke insists that this love is not confined to emotional sentiment but must be demonstrated through *sincere and true* obedience, worship, and a zeal for God's glory. Experimental piety is evident when the believer actively seeks to know and do the will of God, taking delight in His law and finding satisfaction in communion with Him. As Jesus declared, "If ye love me, keep my commandments," (John 14:15). Tuke places this command at the heart of his call to practical holiness, reminding his readers that love is authenticated by action.

Humility, as Tuke portrays it, is the foundation of this love. Pride, the antithesis of humility, blinds the soul to its dependence on God and poisons relationships with others. Experimental piety manifests in the humble recognition of one's unworthiness before God and the extension of grace and service to fellow believers. "God resisteth the proud, but giveth grace unto the humble," (James 4:6) becomes a governing principle for Christian conduct. True humility, Tuke argues, not only acknowledges God's sovereignty but actively seeks to reflect His character through selflessness and compassion.

In practical terms, Tuke exhorts Christians to cultivate love and humility in community, where experimental piety becomes visible. Acts of service, generosity, and forgiveness are not optional extras but essential fruits of a faith that is alive. The Christian home, the local church, and even secular workplaces become arenas where God's grace is made manifest through His people. For Tuke, the greatest evidence of God's work in a soul is its readiness to love and its willingness to bow low in humility. These practices, rooted in grace and fueled by experiential knowledge of God, transform not only the believer but the world around them, serving as a witness to the Lord's goodness and glory.

Conclusion: A Legacy of Holiness and Hope

Thomas Tuke's work concludes with a resounding call to embrace a legacy of holiness and hope, firmly rooted in God's grace and the believer's faithful response. The enduring message of his work challenges Christians to live in the tension between divine sovereignty and Christian responsibility. Through love for God, humility before Him, and a faithful life of service, believers reflect the holiness of their Creator and

Redeemer, leaving behind a testimony of grace that endures beyond their days.

Tuke reminds us that holiness is not an unattainable ideal but a daily pursuit empowered by the Holy Spirit (and it is *discernable*). The faithful saint's life, marked by humility, love, and submission, is a light that shines into the darkness of a pride-filled world. It declares the power of God's grace to redeem, preserve, and transform. Such a life inspires hope, not only for the individual believer but for the entire community of faith, as it points to the promise of eternal life in Christ.

In the end, Tuke's work is an invitation to see one's life as a mirror reflecting God's holiness. The legacy of a Christian is not found in earthly accolades or temporal success but in the consistent witness of a heart surrendered to the Lord. With eyes fixed on God's promises, believers can rest in the assurance that their faithfulness will bear fruit, and their hope in Christ will not be in vain. "Love ye the LORD, all his saints," (Psalm 31:23) remains the rallying cry of a life well-lived in God's glory.

In Christ's grace and mercy,
C. Matthew McMahon, Ph.D., Th.D.
From My study, January, 2025
"...search the Scriptures..." (John 5:39).
www.apuritansmind.com
www.puritanpublications.com

The Mirror of the Soul

www.gracechapeltn.com
www.reformedsynod.com

Meet Thomas Tuke

By C. Matthew McMahon, Ph.D., Th.D.

Thomas Tuke (d. 1657), a royalist clergyman, distinguished himself as a devoted minister and prolific writer during the tumultuous years of early modern England. He pursued his education at Christ's College, Cambridge, earning a Bachelor of Arts degree in 1599 and completing his Master of Arts in 1603. His clerical career began in earnest as the "minister of God's word" at St. Giles-in-the-Fields, London, in 1616. On July 19, 1617, Tuke was appointed by King James I as the vicar of St. Olave Jewry in London. He faithfully served in this position until March 16, 1643, when he was sequestered, plundered, and imprisoned for his unwavering allegiance to the royalist cause during the English Civil War (as recorded in *Mercurius Rusticus*, p. 256). Despite these trials, Tuke continued his ministry and was preaching at Tattershall, Lincolnshire, by 1651.

Richard Smyth's *Obituary* (p. 45) notes that "on September 13, 1657, old Mr. Thomas Tuke, once minister at St. Olave's in the Old Jury, was buried at the new chapel by the new market place in Lincoln's Inn Fields." His wife, Mary, predeceased him and was buried at St. Olave's on June 17, 1654.

Principal Works

Meet Thomas Tuke

Tuke's writings reveal his theological depth and his engagement with pressing religious and moral questions of his time. Many of his works are rare, but they remain significant contributions to 17th-century Christian thought. Below is a list of his principal works, with expanded descriptions for clarity:

1. *A Christian and Plain Treatise of Predestination* (1606, 8vo) Co-translated with Francis Cacot, this work is a translation of William Perkins's treatise on predestination, reflecting the Reformed theological emphasis on divine sovereignty and election.
2. *The True Trial and Turning of a Sinner* (1607, 8vo) A guide for personal repentance and spiritual renewal, emphasizing the transformative power of grace in the life of a believer.
3. *The Treasure of True Love* (1608, 12mo) This work vividly depicts the love of Christ for His Church, using the metaphor of Christ as a bridegroom tenderly devoted to His bride.
4. *The Highway to Heaven* (1609, 8vo) A theological exposition on the doctrines of election, effectual calling, justification, sanctification, and eternal life. A Dutch translation by H. Hexham was published in Dordrecht in 1611.

5. *The Picture of a True Protestant* (1609, 8vo) This text examines the duties and dignities of Christians, both ministers and laity, using agricultural metaphors to describe God's work in His "house and husbandry."
6. *A Very Christian, Learned, and Brief Discourse Concerning the True, Ancient, and Catholic Faith* (1611, 12mo) Translated from the Latin of St. Vincent of Lérins, this discourse defends the continuity of Christian orthodoxy.
7. *A Discourse of Death* (1613, 4to) A meditation on mortality, addressing soldiers, sailors, travelers, expectant mothers, and others, encouraging a thoughtful consideration of death in its various forms.
8. *The Practice of the Faithful* (1613, 8vo) A compilation of devout prayers intended to guide believers in their daily spiritual disciplines.
9. *New Essays: Meditations and Vows* (1614, 12mo) A devotional work exploring the chief duties of Christians in both faith and conduct.
10. *The Christian's Looking-Glass* (this current volume, 1615, 8vo) A reflective guide intended to inspire believers to examine their lives in light of their Christian profession.[1]

---

[1] The Christians LOOKING-GLASSE: Wherein he may clearly see, His love to God lively expressed, His Fidelity truly discovered, and

11. *A Treatise Against Painting and Tincturing of Men and Women* (1616, 4to) A fiery critique of societal vanity, addressing issues such as ambition, pride, and moral corruption. It includes *The Picture of a Picture*, a satirical "character of a painted woman," first published as a broadside.
12. *Index Fidei et Religionis* (1617, 4to) A theological commentary on the first two chapters of the Epistle of James, providing a deep exegetical study.
13. *A Theological Discourse of the Gracious and Blessed Conjunction of Christ and a Sincere Christian* (1617, 8vo) This work explores the intimate relationship between Christ and believers, offering profound insights into union with Christ.
14. *Concerning the Holy Eucharist and the Popish Breaden-God* (1625, 4to; 2nd ed. 1636) Written in verse, this polemical text critiques Roman Catholic views of the Eucharist. It was later reprinted with annotations by Rev. Alexander B. Grosart in 1872.

Pride against God and Man, Anatomized. whereby the Hypocrisy of the times is notoriously manifested. By THOMAS TUKE, Minister of God's Word at Saint Giles in the Fields. (LONDON, Printed by Nicholas Okes, and are to be sold by Richard Bolton, at his Shop in Chancerylane, near Holborne), 1615.

15. *The Israelites' Promise or Profession Made to Joshua* (1651, 8vo) A devotional work reflecting on the covenantal commitments of God's people, using the biblical example of Israel's promise to Joshua.

Thomas Tuke's contributions to theology, pastoral ministry, and polemics reflect the challenges and complexities of his era. His works are cited in several key bibliographies and collections, including the British Museum Library, the Bodleian Library, and *Walker's Sufferings of the Clergy*. Scholars have continued to reference his writings for their historical and theological value.

Sources:
- *Mercurius Rusticus*
- *Obituary* by Richard Smyth
- Bodleian Catalog
- *Hazlitt's Handbook and Collections*
- *Notes and Queries*, 2nd ser. xii. 521
- *Walker's Sufferings of the Clergy*, vol. ii. p. 178.

Themes of the Work

- A description of love in general.
- The nature of good, either true or merely apparent, as the object of love.
- The unifying and joining property of love.
- A detailed exploration of man's love for God.
- The nature of love as an affection of the heart.
- The gracious quality of love.
- The origins of love in knowledge and faith.
- Love as a celestial fire.
- The role of the Holy Ghost in kindling love.
- How love unites us with God and makes Him our ultimate contentment.
- The necessity of loving God demonstrated in six ways.
- The equity of loving God shown in six respects.
- God's love for us described as descending love.
- Six benefits that arise from love for God.
- Nine ways in which love is shown to be excellent.
- Discussion on the author, nature, ends, effects, subjects, and object of love.
- Five reasons why God is more worthy of love than all other things.
- The significance of the terms Jehovah, Kurios, Dominus, and the English word Lord.
- Reasons why the world should not be loved.
- Why riches must not hold our heart.
- On the love of pleasures and why they seem so appealing.

- The uncertainty of honors.
- The vanity of physical beauty.
- How a man may love himself rightly, and who qualifies as such.
- Nine undeniable tokens of true love for God.
- The duty to love God in His universal Church and in every true visible society of believers.
- Identifying what constitutes a true visible Church.
- The obligation to love God in His ministers.
- Reasons to love a minister for their office, authority, labor, and faithful execution of their duties.
- Identifying the marks of a true minister of God.
- The requirement to love God in His people.
- How ministers should demonstrate their love for God by feeding their flocks.
- The necessity of loving God in Christ.
- Reasons why Christ ought to be loved.
- Two special ways of demonstrating love for Christ.
- The meaning of faithfulness in two respects.
- Examples of those who have been considered faithful to the Lord.
- How God preserves the faithful externally.
- How God preserves the faithful internally.
- How God preserves the faithful eternally.
- Three reasons to remain faithful.
- Five distinguishing marks of a faithful person.
- The characteristics of a true Christian.

Themes of the Work

- A commendation of love, illustrated through its notable effects.
- Various similes to demonstrate the worthiness of love.
- The definition of pride.
- Seven ways pride manifests itself in opposition to God.
- How pride against other people reveals itself.
- Twenty-three examples of God's judgments against the proud.
- Two milder forms of God's punishments for pride.
- The folly, baseness, inhumanity, impiety, and injustice of pride.
- The contentious, unsightly, and wasteful nature of pride.
- Pride compared to a thief, thunder, a venomous beast, a moth, or a worm.
- Guidance on how to avoid pride.
- An exhortation to the love of God.
- Assurance that, if God loves us, we need not fear the ill will of men, illustrated by two comparisons.

Introductory Letter

To the Right Virtuous and Honorable Lady, the Lady Alicia Dudley,

Madam,

Three virtues are essential for every Christian to cultivate: charity, fidelity, and humility toward both God and humanity. As the Scripture teaches, "Call no man your father upon the earth: for one is your Father, which is in heaven," (Matthew 23:9).

Among the numerous reasons to love God, four are particularly compelling. First, He is our gracious Father, who, by His own will, brought us into being through the word of truth, making us the first fruits of His creation. If earthly children are bound to love their fathers, from whom they receive part of their physical being, how much more ought we to love God, who gave us our very souls and sustains both soul and body in their entirety? King David acknowledges this when he declares, "Thou hast possessed my reins, thou hast covered me in my mother's womb. Upon thee have I been stayed from the womb, thou art he that took me out of my mother's bowels," (Psalm 139:13; Psalm 22:10). Similarly, Job testifies, "Thine hands have made me and fashioned me together round about; ... Thou hast clothed me with skin and flesh, and hast fenced me with bones and sinews. Thou hast granted me life and favour, and thy visitation hath preserved my spirit," (Job 10:8, 11-12).

Second, we should love God for His exceedingly kind and pleasing nature. This sweetness, though imperceptible to the wicked, remains undiminished. As Isidore observes, those consumed by the fever of iniquity have dulled the palate of their hearts, rendering them incapable of tasting His goodness.

Third, God has earned our love through His boundless beneficence. Out of His immeasurable love, He sent His only Son into the world to rescue us from our lost estate, redeem us from captivity, and grant us life through His death, though we had merited only condemnation.

Fourth, even nature itself compels us to love God. "Ask now the beasts, and they shall teach thee; and the fowls of the air, and they shall tell thee: or speak to the earth, and it shall teach thee: and the fishes of the sea shall declare unto thee," (Job 12:7-8). All creation proclaims His praise and demonstrates its service to mankind, for whose benefit it was made. If animals and the natural world testify to God's goodness, shall man, who alone bears His image, refuse to love Him? Shall we remain indifferent to the One for whom all creatures labor and suffer? As the psalmist writes, "Thou madest him to have dominion over the works of thy hands; thou hast put all things under his feet: all sheep and oxen, yea, and the beasts of the field; the fowl of the air, and the fish of the sea," (Psalm 8:6-8).

The manner of loving God is *no* less important. As humans possess life like plants, senses like animals, and rational understanding unique to mankind, so we must love God with all these faculties. Our Savior commands, "Thou shalt love the Lord thy God with all thy heart, and with all thy soul, and with all thy mind," (Matthew 22:37). To love Him with all our heart means directing all our affections toward Him, delighting in Him above all else. He who loves anything more than God does not truly love God. As St. Augustine states, "Minus te amat, qui aliquid tecum amat quod non propter te amat"—"(*He loves you less, who loves something else with you, which he does not love for your sake.*)"

The tree whose lower branches spread excessively grows less toward the heavens; likewise, the more a man loves earthly things, the less his heart is lifted to God. Such misplaced affections must be pruned, like superfluous branches, so that love for God may flourish. God commands, "My son, give me thine heart," (Proverbs 23:26). He demands the whole heart, for He alone created it, sustains it, and satisfies it. As Augustine also remarks, "Totum exigit te, qui fecit te totum," ("*He who made all of you requires all of you.*") If we owe ourselves entirely to God for our creation, how much more for our redemption? In creation, He gave us to ourselves; in redemption, He gave Himself to us and restored us to ourselves. Being doubly indebted, we owe Him our all.

Furthermore, we are to love God with all our soul. This means valuing God above life itself, preferring to part with the body rather than with Him who is the soul of our soul and the source of all comfort. Our lives should reflect our love for Him, guided by His will, even if it costs us all earthly pleasures and faculties.

Lastly, we must love Him with all our mind, focusing our thoughts on Him and governing our understanding by His Word. A mind informed by divine truth directs the will, affections, and actions toward Him. In this way, we may declare with the apostle, "I live; yet not I, but Christ liveth in me," (Galatians 2:20).

Turning to the love of man, we are called to love ourselves rightly and to love our neighbors as ourselves. To love oneself rightly is to reject sin, for "he that sinneth against me wrongeth his own soul," (Proverbs 8:36). True self-love seeks God's glory and our sanctification. As Augustine notes, "Si male amaveris, tunc odisti: si bene odisti, tunc amasti"—"If you love yourself wrongly, you hate yourself; if you hate yourself rightly, you love yourself." Thus, self-love must be subordinated to love for God.

In loving our neighbors, we must regard all people—friends and enemies, rich and poor, young and old—with charity. As Augustine states, "Per amorem

Dei amor proximi gignitur, et per amorem proximi amor Dei nutritur"—("*The love of God begets the love of neighbor, and the love of neighbor nourishes the love of God.*") To despise Christ in the poor is to fail to love Him in the rich. Indeed, we are commanded to love even our enemies, as Christ teaches, "Love your enemies, bless them that curse you, do good to them that hate you, and pray for them which despitefully use you, and persecute you," (Matthew 5:44).

Let this be the measure of our love for our neighbors: not in quantity but in quality—holily, justly, truly, and consistently. Holily, for God's sake and not against Him; justly, by hating sin while loving the sinner; truly, by seeking their good above all else; and consistently, remaining steadfast in our affection regardless of circumstances.

These virtues—charity, fidelity, and humility—are more fully treated in this book, which I dedicate to your Ladyship. May God, who has already blessed you with these graces, continue to increase them and, in His time, crown you with eternal glory.

From St. Giles in the Fields, August 13, 1614,
Your servant in Christ Jesus,
THOMAS TUKE

PART 1: Exploring Psalm 31

Psalm 31:23, "Love ye the LORD, all his saints: for the LORD preserveth the faithful, and plentifully rewardeth the proud doer."

Holy David, having declared in the preceding four verses the goodness of God toward those who fear Him—especially as experienced in his own life—now exhorts all saints, those sanctified to God by His mercies, to devote and bind themselves to the Lord through love.

In this verse, two aspects are notable: first, the Psalmist's exhortation: "Love ye the LORD, all his saints," and second, the reasons to support this command, drawn from God's grace toward the faithful and His justice toward the proud, as expressed in the following words.

The exhortation involves three key elements:
1. The duty required: Love.
2. The object of that love: The LORD.
3. The persons addressed: All His saints.

Love is described as *"an affection of union"* (*Amor est affectus unionis*), by which we are either united with the beloved or strive to maintain that union. It is "a certain movement of the heart," toward that which is perceived as either truly or apparently good, desiring to draw that good to oneself for enjoyment. The object of love is always some form of good, even when what is loved is mistakenly perceived as good. The nature of love is to unite and bind together, making diverse things one. True, sincere love is distinguished by its focus on that which is good in itself, rather than any self-serving or base motive.

With this pure and sincere love, we are commanded to love God and our neighbor, not for personal gain but for God's sake. The love we are called to have for the Lord is described as a *holy affection* by which we love God in Christ for His own sake. It is "a gracious affection of the heart," born out of knowledge and faith in God, kindled by the Holy Spirit, and binding the soul to God, finding joy and contentment in Him above all else.

This love is an affection of the heart. Love arises from the heart, which is its seat and center. Affections are the movements of the heart, inclining it toward the object of desire.

It is a gracious affection. While love is a natural human capacity, to love rightly—to love the Lord, who is truly good—is the work of grace (χάρις, a gift of divine favor). As the apostle reminds us, "Not that we are sufficient of ourselves to think anything as of ourselves; but our sufficiency is of God," (2 Corinthians 3:5). It is God's grace that empowers us to love rightly, as He "worketh in us both to will and to do of his good pleasure," (Philippians 2:13).

It arises from knowledge and faith. As the maxim states, *Quod latet, ignotum est, ignoti nulla cupido*—"What is unknown is unappreciated, and what is unappreciated cannot be loved." A man cannot love God without first knowing that He exists, that He is good, and that He is deserving of love. Love for God grows in proportion to our knowledge of Him and His benefits.

Because our knowledge of God in this life is imperfect, our love is *also* imperfect. Yet in the world to come, when we "shall see face to face" and "know even as also [we] are known" (1 Corinthians 13:12), our love will be perfected. To illustrate, consider a child who prefers a simple trinket to silver, not knowing its value. Likewise, many fail to love learning or virtue because they are ignorant of their worth. But when a soul comprehends the danger of sin, it begins to hate it; and when it perceives the beauty of true religion, it embraces and loves it.

Similarly, the failure to love God stems from ignorance of His nature and benefits. If men truly understood God's perfections, He would captivate their hearts. Yet the allure of worldly pleasures, profits, and honors often blinds us, raising a fog that obscures His beauty. Let us clear these clouds through diligent seeking, that knowledge may prepare the way for love, as a needle prepares the way for the thread.

It is kindled by faith. Faith assures the believer of God's love, which in turn inspires love for Him. A man who believes only in God's wrath will flee from Him as from an enemy, murmuring and rebelling against Him. But when he is persuaded of God's mercy and reconciled favor, he draws near in love, placing God above all else. The stronger his faith, the stronger his love. Such a soul can echo David's words: "Thou art my Lord: the portion of mine inheritance," (Psalm 16:5). Or again: "Bless the LORD, O my soul, and all that is within me, bless his holy name. Who forgiveth all thine iniquities; who healeth all thy diseases; who redeemeth thy life from destruction; who crowneth thee with lovingkindness and tender mercies," (Psalm 103:1-4).

The apostle Paul affirms that love springs from "a pure heart, and of a good conscience, and of faith unfeigned," (1 Timothy 1:5). Without genuine faith, there can be no pure heart or good conscience.

This truth is also reflected in human relationships. We do not form bonds of love with those we distrust but rather avoid them. Conversely, confidence and trust foster love and delight. Just as one flame ignites another, love begets love. However, if love is not reciprocated, it is often because the recipient does not perceive or acknowledge the affection.

Faith in God is therefore essential. As we grow in faith, our love for Him deepens. Without it, we cannot truly love God as His children. Just as Joseph's brothers did not love him as their brother until he revealed himself and reassured them, so we cannot love God as our Father until, by faith, we are persuaded of His love for us.

Fourthly, I stated that love is kindled in the soul. The love of God is a celestial fire that serves to comfort and refresh the heart, to inflame it with holy zeal, and to consume the foul vapors of malice, envy, pride, treachery, and other vile lusts that reside within.

Fifthly, I affirm that this love is kindled by the Holy Spirit. Saint Paul calls it the fruit of the Spirit, for if hatred of God is a work of the flesh and a motion inspired by the Devil, then true love for God must necessarily be the work of the Spirit. The Spirit enlightens the mind, inspires faith, and persuades the heart to love and delight in God. How greatly we are indebted to God! Out of His pure love for us arises our ability to love Him. He reaches down to us before we rise to Him; He draws us before we run to Him; He gazes upon us before we turn our eyes toward Him. "LORD, what is man, that thou takest knowledge of him! or the son of man, that thou makest account of him?" (Psalm 144:3). What can I render unto the LORD for all His benefits toward me? O my God and my King, I will extol Thee and bless Thy name forever and ever.

Finally, I observed that love knits our hearts to God and causes a man to take Him as his chief contentment. Hatred tears apart, disjoins, and separates, while love unites, knits, and ties together. Love united Jacob and Rachel; love bound David and Jonathan. Likewise, love weds and unites our hearts to God and, through God, to one another. Saint Paul writes, "That their hearts might be comforted, being knit together in love," (Colossians 2:2). It was love that caused our Savior to pray that all His members might be one with Him and His Father. It is also love that moves us to deny ourselves and the world, so that we live as though we are not our own but God's. Hatred breeds dislike, aversion, and discontent, while love fosters joy, delight, and satisfaction.

When love possesses the soul, it stirs it to rejoice in God, to make Him its highest contentment, and to echo the psalmist's words: "Whom have I in heaven but thee? and there is none upon earth that I desire beside thee. My flesh and my heart faileth: but God is the strength of my heart, and my portion for ever," (Psalm 73:25-26). Whatever a man loves most will undoubtedly be his greatest contentment, for love creates contentment just as light brings comfort. Contentment is encased in love, as a tree is encased in its bark or water is held in the clouds. The Greek word for "love" (ἀγαπᾶν) also signifies resting in or being satisfied.

PART 2:
The Object of Love

The object of the love discussed here is the LORD, the One who is gracious and merciful, slow to anger, righteous in all His ways, and holy in all His works. He is the One whose greatness is beyond comprehension and whose wisdom is infinite. He made the heavens, the earth, the sea, and all that is in them. He keeps faith forever, executes justice for the oppressed, gives bread to the hungry, loves the righteous, heals the brokenhearted, preserves all who love Him, fulfills the desires of those who fear Him, defends the fatherless and the widow, and shows mercy to thousands who love Him.

He is the One who remembered us in our low estate, broke the cords of the wicked, rescued us from our oppressors, delivered us from our sins, brought us out of error, led us out of Babylon, and saved us from the Scarlet Harlot. He has given us His Word, bestowed His Gospel upon us, honored us with peace, delivered our rulers, saved His anointed, and preserved both His Church and His kingdom from that hellish and horrific Gunpowder Plot. O LORD, how great is Thy love for us! How glorious is Thy name throughout the earth! Blessed be Thy name forever, and let all Thy people say, Amen.

The persons exhorted *to love* in this passage are all God's saints—all who have tasted His love and whom

He has sanctified by His mercy. This includes all people—young and old, rich and poor, high and low, men, women, and children. By saying "all," none are excluded. The young are called for their strength, the old for their wisdom, the rich for their resources, the poor for their humility, the high for their dignity, and the low for their simplicity, which often pairs best with virtue and piety. Men are called because of their honor, women because God has honored their sex by bringing forth a Savior through them, and children because of His great care and manifold protection over them. All are included for their sanctification by grace on earth and their eternal salvation in heavenly glory.

Are none but God's saints bound to love the LORD? Certainly, the law obliges all, for all are His creatures, and His goodness extends to all. He is the Savior of all mankind. However, David specifically addresses the saints here—those whom he most delighted in, those in whom he had the greatest hope, and those whom God most dearly loves and honors with His highest favors.

From this, we learn that all people, without exception, are called to *love the LORD*. Yet, as one speaking Greek or Latin to someone unfamiliar with those tongues is like a barbarian to him, so the language of love is foreign and displeasing to one who does not love. It becomes as "sounding brass, or a tinkling cymbal," (1 Corinthians 13:1). Therefore, to understand

and benefit from this teaching on loving God, we must rekindle the dying coals of this heavenly and holy fire within our hearts. As the ear discerns words just as the palate discerns food, let us approach with attentive and discerning ears. Recognizing the goodness of what we hear, let us receive it, digest it, and, like wise hearers, manifest its fruits in our lives and conduct.

First, I assert that it is necessary for us to love the LORD. Woe unto us if we fail to love Him. First, because it is God's explicit command: "Thou shalt love the LORD thy God," (Deuteronomy 6:5). Moses declared, "And now, Israel, what doth the LORD thy God require of thee, but to fear the LORD thy God, to walk in all his ways, and to love him," (Deuteronomy 10:12). Our Savior calls this "the first and great commandment" (Matthew 22:38). The Commander is great, the object of the duty is great, the purpose of the duty is great, and the reward for fulfilling it is great. Even if no other reason were provided but the command itself, it would be sufficient to bind us to this duty. *Sic vult, sic jubet, stet pro ratione voluntas*—("Thus He wills, thus He commands, and His will stands as reason.") The authority of a king, the power of a father, and the rights of a master obligate their subjects, children, and servants to obedience. How much more so, then, are we obligated to obey God, who is our King, Father, and Master, possessing absolute and unchallengeable authority over us? His mere command should suffice to compel and control us.

Secondly, in addition to the command, there is a heavy curse awaiting those who do not love God. While our love for God is not the cause of His blessing but rather a sign of it, our hatred or lack of love does merit His curse. Saint Paul declares, "If any man love not the Lord Jesus Christ, let him be *Anathema Maranatha*," (1 Corinthians 16:22).

Thirdly, without love for God, we cannot truly worship Him. True worship requires love combined *with the duty owed* to a superior. Where there is no love, any service offered is either counterfeit or nonexistent. As he who does not love God cannot worship Him, so neither can he love his neighbor for God's sake. "He that loveth not his brother abideth in death," (1 John 3:14). He who does not love the Father as the Father will not love the Son as the Son or his brother as a child of God, a brother of Christ, and a member of the Church.

To further emphasize the necessity of this duty, consider this: just as iron cannot be shaped unless heated in the fire, and wax cannot be sealed unless warm and soft, so we cannot be properly shaped for God's service until our hearts are inflamed with love. Without this holy fire, the Word, the sacraments, the minister's teaching, preaching, binding, loosing, and blessings will hold no true value for us, nor will we derive any comfort from them.

Imagine a man possessing the love of all humanity, able to speak every language, move mountains, cast out devils, heal diseases, and cure wounds. Suppose he gave all his goods to the poor, suffered for the truth, and performed numerous acts of valor for his country. Yet, without love for God, such a man might rightly echo Saint Paul: "I am nothing," (1 Corinthians 13:2). Thus, we see the *necessity* of loving God.

Second, the *equity* of this duty demands our attention. Almighty God loves us, as evidenced by His electing, redeeming, sanctifying, and preserving us in Christ Jesus, His beloved Son. Therefore, it is only right and just that we demonstrate our love for Him. Moreover, our love for God falls far short in measure when compared to His love for us. God's love descends, while ours ascends; descending love is naturally more vigorous, affectionate, and enduring than ascending love. Parents, for example, love their children more intensely than children love their parents, for reasons rooted in understanding and nature.

God knows us perfectly, while our knowledge of Him is limited. Unlike us, He is free from corruption or moral weakness. Furthermore, we possess nothing in God that might elicit His love as we are drawn to Him by what He has placed within us. We, along with all that is good in us, are entirely His.

God loves us even when we are undeserving—when we are by nature "dead in sins" (Ephesians 2:1), "children of wrath" (Ephesians 2:3), and bring forth "roots of bitterness" and "fruits of injustice." How unjust it would be not to love Him who is inherently lovable and who loves us so *undeservingly!* "What is man, that thou art mindful of him? and the son of man, that thou visitest him?" (Psalm 8:4). How much worse is it for man to show such little regard for God, offering Him neither respect nor love?

If ingratitude between men is intolerable, how much more grievous is it *to be unthankful to God?* To receive daily tokens of His love yet offer no love in return is not only ungrateful but also impious and unjust. Far be it from us to engage in such unthankful conduct! "His heart is hard as oak, not flesh, but flint, who, though unwilling to love first, will not respond to love when it is shown," (*Nimis durus est animus, qui si dilectionem nolit impendere, nolit rependere*).

Out of love, God sent His Son—His only Son, the Son of His love—into the world to save us. He provides fruitful seasons, fills our hearts with gladness, and renews His mercies every morning. To refuse to love Him is not only to wrong God but also to injure ourselves, for "all things work together for good to them that love God," (Romans 8:28).

What reason, then, do we have to desire His love while withholding our own? Can we expect love from our families, neighbors, and acquaintances if we fail to show love to Him who has adopted, redeemed, and united us to Himself? How can we expect respect for our commands from those under us if we neglect this duty, which God so rightly commands and expects from us? Common sense and equity compel us to love Him.

Third, the *benefits* of loving God should inspire us to fulfill this duty. First, love enables faith to produce the good works we owe to God. Faith is the hand that receives, but love is the hand that gives. Without love, no work is truly good. As Saint Paul writes, "Faith worketh by love," (Galatians 5:6). Saint Augustine observes, *Nec faciunt bonos vel malos mores, nisi boni vel mali sint amores*— ("It is good or bad loves that make conduct good or bad.") A holy love produces a holy life, while an earthly love leads to an earthly life. If a man's love is directed toward God, his life will reflect that goodness.

Love also tempers and seasons knowledge. Without love, knowledge becomes vain, prideful, and unfruitful. Saint Paul warns, "Knowledge puffeth up, but charity edifieth," (1 Corinthians 8:1). Just as undigested food corrupts rather than nourishes, so knowledge not infused with love breeds arrogance and harmful dispositions. On the other hand, knowledge warmed and tempered by the sacred fire of love becomes a source of nourishment and strength.

Similarly, the words of instruction, exhortation, and comfort from Scripture, delivered in the ministry of the Church, are unprofitable unless received with love. But when embraced with love, they bear the fruits of righteousness and render us more fruitful and serviceable to God and man. Just as heat transforms rain into fertile soil, so love transforms God's Word *within* us, not merely conforming the Word to us but conforming us to it. Through love, we war against our earthly lusts so that God's Word might reign in peace within us.

O Love, through you I abandon myself so that God's Word might enter in; through you I fight against myself so that it may rule in peace; through you I mortify my earthly members so that it may live and prosper in me!

Thirdly, the love of God *enables* us to *discern* our spiritual condition. A man, by the grace within him, may perceive the grace of God toward him. Just as one can observe the movement of the sun by looking at a sundial, so too, by examining his own soul, a man may understand the goodwill of God toward him. Though I cannot see the air itself, I can feel its effects; likewise, though I cannot see God's heart or His love as it resides in His being, there are clear manifestations of His love in the hearts of men. If a person finds these manifestations in himself, he may rest assured of God's love for him.

The love that a man has for God is a result of God's love for him. He who loves God can conclude that God loves him, for God effectually calls no one except out of His love. As Saint Paul teaches, "To them who are the called according to his purpose," (Romans 8:28). He further says, "If any man love God, the same is known of him," (1 Corinthians 8:3), meaning that such a person is acknowledged, loved, and approved by God. Saint John also writes, "We love him, because he first loved us," (1 John 4:19). Our love for God originates in His love for us, just as rivers flow from the sea. His love draws our hearts to Him as a magnet attracts iron or as the Sardius stone attracts wood. Our love mirrors His love, as an echo responds to a voice or as a reflection corresponds to the face in water: "As in water face answereth to face, so the heart of man to man," (Proverbs 27:19). Similarly, as one candle lights another, so the recognition of God's love for us kindles our love for Him. This reflection of our love is itself a gracious operation of His love within us, not a product of the flesh, which is opposed to God, but of the Spirit, which proceeds from Him.

Those who hate God and love the things of this world belong to Babylon, the domain of the devil, while those who love God are citizens of Jerusalem, the Catholic Church, our mother, and belong to God, our Father. They are forgiven of their sins. Let every man ask himself what he loves, and by doing so, he shall discover the state of his soul and to which city he *belongs*. It is true that a man is not loved by God because he loves Him; rather, he loves God *because God first loved him*. Just as the sun's rays shining upon a silver plate produce heat and light, so too does God's love, shining upon us, inflame our hearts with love. This love moves us to good affection not only toward God but also, for His sake, toward others. Like the heat radiating from a silver plate, our love for God inspires and impacts all who come into contact with us.

Fourthly, the love of God is *not idle*; if it does not produce action, it is not love. True love for God compels us to love the godly for God's sake, which is both natural and comforting. Just as one who loves a king cannot help but love his loyal subjects, and one who loves a father cannot hate his child, so too, one who loves God will love those who exhibit godly behavior and show themselves to be His servants and children. These individuals are the most vivid reflections of God that mortals can see. This love is comforting because it assures us that we are true disciples of our Lord and confirms, as the Apostle teaches, that we are "translated from death unto life," (1 John 3:14).

Just as many branches spring from one root and much water flows from one source, so many virtues arise from this love. As Gregory says, *Non habet viriditatem ramus boni operis, nisi manserit in radice charitatis*—("The branch of good works has no greenness unless it remains in the root of charity.") Without the nourishment of love, all virtues will wither. The love of money, or mammon, is the root of all evil (1 Timothy 6:10); in contrast, the love of God is the source and sustainer of all good, inspiring both piety toward God and Christian charity toward man.

Part 2: The Object of Love

In a word, the love of God is as strong as death. Just as death destroys the body, so *love for God mortifies our love for the world.* Like a strong wind dispersing thick and foul-smelling fogs of rancor, wrath, and malice, the love of God clears away these corrupt affections. As the rising sun drives out the cold and lethargy of the night, and as wine poured into a vessel displaces the air within it, so the love of God drives out the inordinate love of worldly vanities. Once our hearts are warmed with His love, the coldness of our affections toward good things departs. When God enters the heart, mammon must leave. Fixing our eyes on heaven removes them from earth, and entering into a covenant of love with God causes us to fall out of love with, and into hatred for, all His enemies. As David says, "Do not I hate them, O LORD, that hate thee? ... I count them mine enemies," (Psalm 139:21-22). Thus, we see the benefits of this love for God.

PART 3:
The Excellence of Love

The excellence of this love remains to be discussed. True love for God is excellent for the following reasons:

1. **Its Author**: The author of this love is not man but God Himself. As Saint John teaches, "Love is of God; and every one that loveth is born of God, and knoweth God," (1 John 4:7). Whoever loves God does so by God's grace and gift.

2. **Its Ends**: The purposes of this love are honorable, not base. These include the glory of God, the salvation of our souls, the edification of our brothers, the honor of our calling, and the prevention of grieving the Spirit of God.

3. **Its Cause**: The reason for our love is God's goodness—His intrinsic goodness and His goodness to us.

4. **Its Subjects**: This love resides only in God's saints and servants, the most excellent among humanity. In them, it is the heart—man's noblest part—that serves as the altar upon which this heavenly fire, kindled by the Holy Ghost, burns.

5. **Its Attendants**: Love is not solitary but accompanied by all virtues, much like an honorable lady who is well attended.

Part 3: The Excellence of Love

6. **Its Perpetuity**: Love surpasses faith and hope in endurance. When faith and hope are fulfilled in the enjoyment of their objects, they will cease, but love will not. Instead, love will be perfected and continue eternally.
7. Seventhly, our love for God has three most excellent effects, to speak of no more.

First, love makes a man diligent in his service to God and, for God's sake, to others. True obedience is the fruit of love, and any obedience not born of love is hypocritical and without savor. The love of a child compels him to obey his father, even if the father lacks the power to punish. Similarly, the love of a child of God moves him to serve God freely, even without the fear of punishment or the promise of reward. Such is the power of love that it makes a man obey God simply for the sake of obedience, without thought of heaven or hell. Among men, love drives one to do good for another, even when there is no prospect of repayment.

Secondly, love makes a man like God, for "God is love," (1 John 4:8). It is no small honor for a child to resemble his father, and so it is with the children of God who imitate Him in their love.

Thirdly, the one who loves God surrenders himself entirely to God, giving up self-interest and self-reliance. By degrees, he dies to himself, and God, whom he loves, lives in him. This love is of such a transforming nature that the lover is drawn out of himself, forgets himself, and denies himself entirely, becoming wholly absorbed in God. Saint Paul captures this transformation when he says, "I am crucified with Christ: nevertheless I live; yet not I, but Christ liveth in me," (Galatians 2:20). Just as the love of the world makes the worldling live for the world and the world for him, so the love of God causes the believer to live for God, and God, in turn, dwells in him. Thus, the believer is no longer his own but belongs to God. "Not ours, but His," (*Non nostra sed sua*).

Eighthly, our love for God is excellent because of the incomparable reward God has promised to those who love Him. This reward is nothing less than a crown and a kingdom: the crown of glory and the kingdom of heaven. Saint James writes, "Hath not God chosen the poor of this world rich in faith, and heirs of the kingdom which he hath promised to them that love him?" (James 2:5). Similarly, Saint Paul declares that the "crown of righteousness" will be given to those who love Christ's appearing (2 Timothy 4:8). Only those who love Him can truly look forward to His return, for no one can eagerly anticipate the coming of a judge unless he loves the Judge.

He who would reign in heaven must *first* love God on earth. He who desires heavenly glory must first possess this grace. How men love the fleeting pleasures of this world, which are imperfect and temporary! Yet, "in thy presence is fulness of joy; at thy right hand there are pleasures for evermore," (Psalm 16:11). Men are eager for riches and crowns, though "riches are not for ever: and doth the crown endure to every generation?" (Proverbs 27:24). The riches and glory that come through the love of God are eternal and unchanging. Earthly pleasures and treasures may dazzle the eyes of fools, but "eye hath not seen, nor ear heard, neither have entered into the heart of man, the things which God hath prepared for them that love him," (1 Corinthians 2:9). These blessings are beyond expression, comprehensible only to those who experience them.

Let us, therefore, set our love on God and remove it from the world. To love God is to love the One who rewards with unparalleled honor, while to love the world is to embrace a betrayer. The world says to the devil of its lovers, as Judas said to the Jews, "Whomsoever I shall kiss, that same is he: hold him fast," (Matthew 26:48). Like Jael to Sisera, the world lulls its lovers to sleep with comforts, only to drive a nail through their temples (Judges 4:21).

Finally, the love of God is excellent because of its object—God Himself. He is omnipotent, omnipresent, omniscient, all-wise, eternal, and ever-loving. He is goodness, mercy, justice, love, and life itself. He is the perfection of all virtues, the beauty of beauties. In Hebrew, He is called Jehovah, meaning "He who is" or "He who exists in and of Himself," while all other things exist from and for Him. In Greek, He is *Kyrios*, "the one with authority over all." In Latin, He is *Dominus*, "the one who tames, rules, and owns all things." In English, He is the "Lord," derived from "*Il-laf-ford*," meaning "a giver" or "a provider of bread," for He gives sustenance to all living creatures and provides for both their temporal and eternal needs.

The excellence of God should compel us to love Him. Who is as great, as sweet, or as worthy of love as God? Is your delight in might? "Behold, I am the LORD, the God of all flesh: is there any thing too hard for me?" (Jeremiah 32:27). Does your heart admire wisdom? God is all-knowing, confounding the plans of the wicked and wise in their own conceits, (Job 5:12-13). Do you esteem strength? "The LORD strong and mighty, the LORD mighty in battle," (Psalm 24:8). Even the strength of angels and the courage of all creatures combined is but a drop compared to His infinite power.

Is your admiration reserved for those who perform wonders? "He doeth great things and unsearchable; marvellous things without number," (Job 5:9). He "stretcheth out the heavens as a curtain, and spreadeth them out as a tent to dwell in," (Isaiah 40:22). Do you seek faithfulness? God is faithful, "keeping his covenant and mercy to them that love him and keep his commandments," (Deuteronomy 7:9). Do you desire righteousness? "The LORD is righteous in all his ways, and holy in all his works," (Psalm 145:17).

Do you *value* mercy? "The LORD is gracious, and full of compassion," (Psalm 145:8). He provides strength to the weak and opens the ears of the afflicted in their troubles (Job 36:15).

God's excellence surpasses all comprehension. If we value truth, constancy, and unchanging love, let us love the LORD, for "with whom is no variableness, neither shadow of turning," (James 1:17). His love is everlasting, and He never fails to do good for those who are His. "He will not fail thee, nor forsake thee," (Deuteronomy 31:6). Those He loves, He loves forever.

The truth is, there is no man or anything in the world that deserves our love as God does, nor anything that should rival Him in our affections.

First, we may love others and not receive their love in return. Often, the more some are loved, the less they reciprocate, disliking even those who love them most. In contrast, the more a man loves God, the more he may be assured of God's love—not because our love earns His, but because our love is a fruit of His love for us. As the heat radiating from a wall or ground testifies to the sun shining upon it, so our love for God reflects the beams of His love toward us.

Secondly, earthly things, such as riches, honor, credit, and promotions, cannot provide the satisfaction that God offers. They are fleeting and uncertain, while God is eternal and unchanging. These things often come with elements that displease or harm us, but God is entirely good, wholly profitable, and a source of pure pleasure. One may become weary or overindulge in worldly possessions, loving them excessively to his own ruin. But no one can have too much of God, nor can anyone love Him too greatly or for too long. The measure of loving God is to love Him without measure; it is a perpetual debt that can never be fully repaid. Even if a man possessed all the pleasures, wealth, and honor the world could provide, his restless heart would still crave more, for the world is round and finite, while the human heart is triangular and insatiable—like fire that never says, "It is enough." If a man finds contentment in earthly things, it is not because they satisfy, but because he recognizes their insufficiency. Only God, the fullness of all good, truth, beauty, and perfection, can truly satisfy the soul—no matter how many worlds of souls there might be.

Thirdly, we love men whose power cannot reach the soul and whose love often offers little benefit. But the wrath of God affects *both* body and soul, being far more dreadful than the roar of ten thousand lions. In contrast, "in his favour is life," (Psalm 30:5). His love is the source of holiness, happiness, grace, and glory—the wellspring of all our comfort and contentment.

Fourthly, our love for created things is accompanied by fear and anxiety lest harm befall them. As the poet says, *Res est solliciti plena timoris amor*— ("Love is full of anxious fear.") Friends may die or be injured, possessions stolen, homes destroyed, reputations tarnished, servants corrupted, children mistreated, and spouses betrayed. Earthly things are vulnerable to fire, water, storms, beasts, sin, sickness, men, and devils. But God is beyond all harm; He is blessed, unchanging, invincible, and untouchable. He is above all and dependent on none.

Finally, while some people accept the love of a few and reject the love of others, God shows no partiality. He accepts the love of anyone who loves Him, even though no human love can add to His glory or satisfaction. Among men, love often breeds jealousy, envy, and rivalry. But with God, the grace of love compels us to desire companions in loving Him. A man who aligns himself with another may fear competition from a rival suitor, but God has enough to give to all who love Him. Each one may say, "The lines are fallen unto me in pleasant places; yea, I have a goodly heritage", (Psalm 16:6). "Thou anointest my head with oil; my cup runneth over," (Psalm 23:5). God is pleased when His followers turn others toward Him, increasing His friends. Such a man, laboring out of love, will not lose his reward: "For God is not unrighteous to forget your work and labour of love, which ye have showed toward his name," (Hebrews 6:10). "They that turn many to righteousness shall shine as the stars for ever and ever," (Daniel 12:3).

The apostles were sent into the world to gather disciples for God and to increase His followers.

To press this point further: How can man show gratitude to God unless he loves Him for creating him in His image? How can he excuse himself for failing to love God, who placed him in a world richly furnished with light for seeing, air for breathing, food for nourishment, clothing for covering, and dominion over the fish of the sea, the birds of the air, and every living thing on earth (Genesis 1:28-29)?

We are commanded to have no other gods but the LORD, who delivered us from the bondage of sin and Satan (Exodus 20:3). Yet this command can only be fulfilled through love, which binds and weds us to Him.

How shall we hallow His name and avoid defiling it unless we love it? How shall we forgive injuries without seeking vengeance, if not persuaded by love for God? Who but one who loves God would, like Moses, forgo personal greatness for God's glory (Exodus 32:32)? Who, but through love, would ensure that those in his care do not rebel against Him?

The love of God compels, sustains, and transforms. Without it, gratitude, obedience, and devotion are *impossible*.

How can parents raise their children in the fear of God, instruct them carefully in His commandments, and fulfill their duty to bring them up in the nurture and admonition of the LORD, unless the love of God moves them to do so? Without love for God, this solemn responsibility will neither be undertaken nor carried out as it ought.

How can we meditate on the *Law of God* day and night, as we are exhorted to do, given the natural dullness and aversion of our hearts, unless the love of God overcomes our reluctance and inspires us to obedience?

How can we avoid turning aside, as the children of Israel did, to follow the corrupt inventions of men, or keep ourselves from idolatry when tempted, unless our love for God restrains and governs us?

Who but a soul deeply in love with God will say to Him what Ruth said to Naomi: "Whither thou goest, I will go; and where thou lodgest, I will lodge" (Ruth 1:16)? It is the lack of love that causes men to forsake God, refuse His service, and leave His house.

Would a mother, like Hannah, dedicate her son to the LORD unless her love for Him compelled her? Such an act of devotion, if sincere, is the fruit of her love for God.

Would you, like David, set all the laws of God before you and not depart from them? Would you remain upright and guard yourself from iniquity? Only love for God can motivate such faithfulness. What made Jonathan so loyal to David, saying, "Whatsoever thy soul desireth, I will even do it for thee," (1 Samuel 20:4)? It was love, for he loved David as his own soul.

What but love compelled the true mother to cry out to Solomon, "Slay him not," while the other, devoid of love, heartlessly said, "Divide it" (1 Kings 3:26)? In the same way, only love for God will make a man seek peace and unity in His house and grieve at its division.

What moved Hezekiah to break down idols, cut down groves, and destroy the brazen serpent that had become an object of idolatry? It was zeal born of love for God (2 Kings 18:4). Without such love, no one will cling to the LORD, cast down their personal idols, or keep their soul pure.

Would you willingly bear the cost of true religion and cheerfully offer sacrifices and gifts to God without counting them a burden? Then love must bind your heart to Him. It was this love that made David say to Ornan, "I will not take that which is thine for the LORD, nor offer burnt offerings without cost," (1 Chronicles 21:24). It was love that inspired the Israelites to willingly give their gold, silver, and precious stones for the building of the Temple, offering "willingly to the LORD with a perfect heart," (1 Chronicles 29:9).

Surely it was love for God that led Solomon to pray for wisdom to govern His people and to build a house for the Name of the LORD (2 Chronicles 1:10). It was love that caused David to declare, "I will not come into the tabernacle of my house, nor go up into my bed; I will not give sleep to mine eyes, or slumber to mine eyelids, until I find out a place for the LORD, an habitation for the mighty God of Jacob," (Psalm 132:3-5). Likewise, you, whom Christ has made a spiritual king, must devote yourself to God through love if you would govern your own heart, mortify your lusts, and make your soul a dwelling place for the LORD. If love does not keep you awake, how will you find a place for God to abide in your heart?

Love for God and His worship moved the people to sing for joy and shout when the foundation of the LORD's house was laid (Ezra 3:11). Similarly, we must love God truly if we are to rejoice in seeing His Church established or repaired, whether in a nation, city, village, family, or individual. Only true love for God enables us to rejoice when the truth of Christ is planted and embraced.

We are commanded to sanctify the Sabbath day, as Nehemiah zealously reminded the people: "What evil thing is this that ye do, and profane the sabbath day? Did not your fathers thus, and did not our God bring all this evil upon us, and upon this city? Yet ye bring more wrath upon Israel by profaning the sabbath," (Nehemiah 13:17-18). Unless we sanctify God in our hearts by love, we will never sanctify His Sabbath, and the allure of profit and pleasure will steal from God the devotion owed to Him. It was love that made Esther plead with the king, "How can I endure to see the evil that shall come unto my people? or how can I endure to see the destruction of my kindred?" (Esther 8:6). He who loves Jacob will grieve for the afflictions of Joseph. A heart that loves God cannot remain unmoved by the plots of the wicked against His people. He who could witness the *Powder Plot* without outrage or rejoice in its failure without gratitude is void of love for God.

What enabled Job to endure his trials with patience, saying, "Though he slay me, yet will I trust in him," (Job 13:15)? It was love. What inspired David to declare, "Thou art my LORD: thy law is within my heart," (Psalm 40:8), and to compose so many psalms in praise of God? It was love. What led Agur to pray, "Feed me with food convenient for me: lest I be full, and deny thee, and say, Who is the LORD? or lest I be poor, and steal, and take the name of my God in vain," (Proverbs 30:8-9)? It was love.

What caused Solomon to abandon his lusts, cry out that "all is vanity," and call us to remember God in our youth (Ecclesiastes 12:1)? It was love. What moved the Church to cry out to her Bridegroom, "Let him kiss me with the kisses of his mouth," (Song of Solomon 1:2), and to long for His presence? She was "sick of love," (Song of Solomon 2:5).

What drove Daniel to face the lions, the three Hebrew children to enter the fiery furnace, and the Christian martyrs to endure cruel deaths? It was love. They "loved not their lives unto the death," (Revelation 12:11), valuing God's glory above their own lives, liberties, pleasures, or profits, and holding His truth higher than all earthly things.

What will you love? Wealth and riches? Will you set your heart on that which is fleeting and insubstantial? "Wilt thou set thine eyes upon that which is not? for riches certainly make themselves wings; they fly away as an eagle toward heaven," (Proverbs 23:5). Riches have caused more loss than they have redeemed, and rich men often find themselves surrounded by flatterers rather than true friends. These followers, like ants to grain or crows to carrion, seek the riches, not the man. As the saying goes, *Praedam sequitur ista turba, non hominem*—("Such a crowd follows the prey, not the person.") They value the wealth and care nothing for the one who possesses it. They would strip him of all he has if it served their gain.

An ancient philosopher, upon losing all his wealth, remarked, *Periissem, ni perissem*—("I would have been ruined if I had not lost it.") How much truer is this for God, our greatest good! Whether we lose earthly goods or not, if we lose Him—if we love riches more than Him—we lose everything, including ourselves, our comfort, and our contentment. Therefore, "if riches increase, set not your heart upon them," (Psalm 62:10). If you lack wealth, be content, for "he that loveth silver shall not be satisfied with silver", (Ecclesiastes 5:10). The richest man is he who desires the least, and the greatest is he who finds satisfaction in the smallest portion.

PART 4:
What Do You Love?

What then will have your love? Pleasures? What are pleasures but "vanity of vanities"? What are they compared to the *pain* of hell that follows them or to the *sweetness* found in God? If your soul were truly attuned to the taste of God's love, the pleasures of this world would seem bitter by comparison. That men do not perceive the sweetness of God is because their spiritual taste is corrupted by the sickness of worldly love. Consider Moses, who "chose rather to suffer affliction with the people of God, than to enjoy the pleasures of sin for a season; esteeming the reproach of Christ greater riches than the treasures in Egypt," (Hebrews 11:25-26). Recall Solomon's cautionary words: "Rejoice, O young man, in thy youth; and let thy heart cheer thee in the days of thy youth...but know thou, that for all these things God will bring thee into judgment," (Ecclesiastes 11:9).

Lysimachus, to quench his thirst, surrendered himself to his enemies, the Scythians, only to lament afterward, *Quam brevis voluptatis causa quantam deposui felicitatem!*—("For such a brief pleasure, how much happiness I have lost!") Let us beware of trading our eternal inheritance for fleeting indulgences, as Esau sold his birthright for a mere morsel of food. "Pleasure is the bait of evil, with which men are caught as fish with a hook." Avoid it altogether, or at least take heed of the hidden snare.

What will you love then? Honor? How unstable and fleeting it is! Haman was honored one day and hanged the next (Esther 7:10). Olofernes was a great leader one night and headless by morning (seen in apocryphal book of Judith, 13:8). History is full of examples of sudden falls from honor. He who is esteemed today may be scorned tomorrow. "For the sun is no sooner risen with a burning heat, but it withereth the grass, and the flower thereof falleth, and the grace of the fashion of it perisheth," (James 1:11). Caesar was stabbed at the height of his power, Nebuchadnezzar was humiliated in his greatness, Alexander the Great was poisoned in his prime, and Herod was struck down while the people hailed him as a god (Acts 12:21-23). Honor is like smoke that vanishes while you gaze upon it. How much greater and more enduring are the honors reserved for those who love God!

Perhaps beauty will claim your love. Hear Bathsheba's wisdom to Solomon: "Favour is deceitful, and beauty is vain: but a woman that feareth the LORD, she shall be praised," (Proverbs 31:30). What is beauty but a fleeting pleasure for the eye, fragile and temporary? A single wound, an illness, or the passage of a few years can mar it entirely. Bion called it *Bonum alienum*—("a good not truly ours.") Socrates described it as a "brief tyranny," and Theophrastus called it a "silent deceiver."

Part 4: What Do You Love?

Without love for God, even the most beautiful person is like a tulip—pleasing to the eye but lacking fragrance—or a gilded potsherd. True beauty lies not in the outward form but in the fear of the LORD. If you admire the gift of beauty, how much more should you adore the Giver, whose beauty surpasses all understanding?

If you do not choose any of these, what then will you love? Yourself? Be cautious, for to idolize yourself is to make yourself your own enemy. Certainly, you may love yourself rightly by loving God in yourself and yourself in God. Love yourself under God, not above Him; for His sake, not against Him. Otherwise, in loving yourself wrongly, you will hate your soul and lose it. "He that loveth his life shall lose it," (John 12:25). God is the soul of your soul, the joy of your heart, the strength of your life, your shield, and your savior. To lose Him is to lose everything.

What shall separate us from the love of God—the Father of our spirits, the breath of our nostrils, the source of our comfort, the rock of our defense, and the fountain of life? Shall riches, pleasures, beauty, honor, tribulations, or even death itself? No, "For I am persuaded, that neither death, nor life, nor angels, nor principalities, nor powers...shall be able to separate us from the love of God, which is in Christ Jesus our Lord," (Romans 8:38-39).

What would it profit you to gain the whole world and lose your own soul? (Matthew 16:26). To be beloved by all men but hated by the God of men? Let us, therefore, love God and keep Him always, for "he that hath God hath everything; and he that hath not God hath nothing."

Because it is essential for every good Christian to love God sincerely, with true and regular affection, and because the human heart is often deceived by its own imaginings—being "a sea of subtlety and a mine of deceit," inclined to mislead itself—it is necessary to establish certain signs by which we may discern whether we truly love God or merely approach Him with outward gestures, while our hearts remain far from Him.

First, true love is not idle but laborious. *Si operari renuerit, amor non est*—("If it refuses to work, it is not love.") What effort will a soldier spare in pursuit of victory? What will the greedy man not do to gain or keep riches? Consider Esther, who labored to save her people, the Jews. Jacob endured the heat of the day, the frost of the night, and sleepless toil in the service of fourteen years under Laban, a harsh master, all for his love of Rachel. Gamblers stay awake night and day over dice and cards. Vanity consumes time and money as women labor endlessly over attire and adornments. Can it then be supposed that the love of God alone is lazy, unwilling to work or endure hardship? Certainly not.

Second, he who loves God truly will love Him for who He is, not merely for His gifts. God is to be loved for

His inherent goodness, excellence, perfection, and beauty, not merely for the tokens of love He bestows. Loving God only for His *blessings* is to love oneself more than God. Many people treat God as they do their friends—not loving them for their virtues but for the benefits they provide. In contrast, Paul declares, "I seek not yours, but you," (2 Corinthians 12:14), and Moses, when offered greatness at the expense of his people, preferred their good over his advancement, interceding for them even at personal cost. He pleaded for God's glory, saying, "Yet now, if thou wilt forgive their sin; and if not, blot me, I pray thee, out of thy book which thou hast written," (Exodus 32:32).

Third, to love God sincerely is to obey Him joyfully, simply because He commands it. Obedience for its own sake demonstrates reverence and affection for the one who issues the command.

Fourth, genuine love allows no rival. The true lover of God dethrones all other attachments—whether wealth, pleasure, self-interest, or human affections—so that God alone may rule within. As a faithful spouse tolerates no rival, so God admits no competition: *Aut Caesar aut nullus*—("Either God is all, or He is nothing.") If nothing diverts your heart from Him, your love is steadfast.

Fifth, as the greedy man's insatiable desire for riches proves his love for wealth, so the true lover of God desires ever greater intimacy with Him. Such a person, like the spouse in the Song of Solomon, exclaims, "I am sick of love," (Song of Solomon 2:5) and is restless until they find full communion with God. Complete satisfaction will only come in heaven, but the longing and "sickness" of the soul here on earth are signs of true love. Just as thirst proves a love for drink, so spiritual longing evidences a love for God.

Sixth, the thoughts of those who love God are continually directed toward Him. As the covetous think of wealth, the ambitious of honor, and the scholars of their books, so the lover of God meditates on His power, providence, justice, mercy, and glory. Love brings the heart into God's presence and keeps it there. David declares, "O how love I thy law! it is my meditation all the day," (Psalm 119:97).

Seventh, constancy in devotion is a mark of true love. The genuine lover of God remains faithful in all seasons—whether in prosperity or adversity, sunshine or storm. Such love is unwavering, enduring trials with courage, and overcoming all difficulties through its strength. The martyrs, through their steadfast love, overcame both temptations and persecutions, remaining unshaken in their devotion to God.

Eighth, obedience to God's commandments is the ultimate evidence of true love. As John writes, "For this is the love of God, that we keep his commandments," (1 John 5:3). A child demonstrates love for a parent through obedience, and a servant shows loyalty by fulfilling his master's will. Similarly, those who truly love God strive to live in accordance with His Word. If someone knowingly continues in sin or values earthly pleasures above God's commands, their love is counterfeit. While outward actions may appear righteous, if they are done without love for God, they are of no value in His sight.

True love for God reforms the heart, shaping every thought, word, and deed to conform to His will. It dethrones competing affections, spurs us to obedience, and sustains us through trials. Let us, therefore, examine ourselves by these marks and seek the grace to love God with all our heart, soul, and strength. Only such love is worthy of the God who has loved us first and given Himself for us.

PART 5:
God Loved in His Church

To conclude, God must be loved in His Church, in His Ministers, in His Children, and most supremely in His beloved Son, Christ Jesus. Those who hate any of these cannot truly love God.

First, God is to be loved in His Church. By "Church," I do not only mean the universal Catholic Church, which is the mother of all true believers and without whose love one cannot claim God as Father, proving themselves a counterfeit plant. I specifically refer to all true visible churches or congregations. True churches are those honored by God with true doctrine, sufficient means of salvation, and ministers with genuine authority to dispense His ordinances. Anyone who loves such a church for what it is—for God and in God—demonstrates their love for God.

He who loves a ring for the diamond it holds or for the skill of the craftsman surely loves both the diamond and the craftsman even more. Similarly, one who loves the Church for her Word, Sacraments, and the power of God within her loves God, whose gracious blessing established her. If we love the Church for being God's Church, we cannot hate God, who is her head.

Conversely, if you hate a true Church of God, how can the love of God dwell in you? You may claim you would not hate her if you were sure she was true.

But if you are not sure, why hate her? If you cannot discern her truth, are you certain of her falseness? If you are unsure, neither hate her nor separate from her. To reject her without clear evidence is folly. Blindness to her truth does not justify your separation, and if others—both near and far—acknowledge her as a true Church, should you not reconsider? Let us show our love for God by loving His Church.

Second, God is to be loved in His Ministers, who are called "Men of God" and "Saints" because of their holy office, which God has sanctified for Himself. Their ministry is not only sacred but sanctifying and salvific. He who loves these saints for their office loves God, the Sanctifier. To love a minister for his work's sake, as Paul exhorts, is to love God, whom the minister serves. However, to despise ministers for faithfully preaching truth, exposing error, or rebuking sin—whether it be pride, drunkenness, profanity, Sabbath-breaking, or neglect of God's ordinances—betrays enmity against God. Those who reject His messengers would reject Him were He to come in their midst.

Do you claim to love your minister? If so, is it because he is *God's* minister, charged with the care of your soul? If you love him for this, your case is good, for you love God. But if you love him only for his wealth, status, or other worldly reasons, that is no sign of love for God. To honor a minister for his faithful work is divine, but to despise or persecute him for fulfilling his calling is devilish and reveals hatred of light and love of darkness. He who hates the servant cannot love the Master. When men reject or dishonor God's ministers, they dishonor God.

But let it be clear: only true and faithful ministers deserve this honor—those who deliver God's message, not their own errors. If they corrupt or distort the Word, or administer the sacraments unfaithfully, they abuse their authority and are to be reproved and avoided.

Third, God is to be loved in His children. All godly men bear God's name, are renewed by His Spirit, and are made holy through His work. To love a godly man for his godliness, a saint for his sanctity, and a believer for his new nature is to love God, the author of these virtues. Conversely, if one claims to love God but hates his brother, he is a liar (1 John 4:20). To hate a brother for his godliness, sobriety, or zeal is to hate God Himself. Thus, Christ said to Saul, "Saul, Saul, why persecutest thou me?" (Acts 9:4). Saul had not persecuted Christ in person but His followers, yet the offense was counted against Christ.

As John writes, "Every one that loveth him that begat loveth him also that is begotten of him," (1 John 5:1). Therefore, to hate those begotten of God is to hate God Himself. Those who despise piety, zeal, or holy living in others cannot excuse themselves of hating God, who is the source of these graces. David speaks of such people as adversaries to their neighbors "because they follow goodness," (Psalm 38:20). Their hatred of Zion and her righteous inhabitants proves their enmity toward God, who will surely judge them. Let such people turn from hatred to love before it is too late.

Let us therefore love God in His Church, in His Ministers, in His Children, and above all in Christ Jesus, for to love these is to love God. Conversely, to hate these is to hate Him who is their source and sustainer. May we guard our hearts against such hatred and devote ourselves wholly to the love of God.

I confess, there is much love in the world—such as it is: natural love, civil love, domestic love, matrimonial love, fleshly love, worldly love, pot-love, and human love. Yet, how little godly charity is evident among us! Who loves godliness in a man? Who seeks God in their neighbor, friend, child, servant, or companion? Who strives to see religion, justice, and true Christianity flourish in their children, servants, friends, and neighbors?

I do not doubt that Turks, Moors, and other pagans sometimes love religious and true Christians, as I believe some of our merchants and their factors—who live and trade among them—are loved. But do they love their religion? Do they love them for their Christianity? No, they do not. They would *prefer* them to be as superstitious as themselves. Therefore, if you wish to give an unmistakable demonstration of your love for God, love your brother for God's sake and in God. Love his piety, his Christianity, and pray earnestly that the kingdom of God may be planted and established in him. Just as all men should demonstrate their love for God by loving His people, ministers of God especially must show this love by diligently and faithfully feeding their flocks. For this reason, our Lord required Peter to express his love for Him by tending His sheep: *"Peter, lovest thou me? Feed my lambs. Feed my sheep. Feed my sheep,"* (John 21:15-17). As Bernard said, "Feed them with your mind, feed them with your mouth, feed them with your deeds—feed them with the prayer of your heart, the exhortation of the Word, and by setting them a good example." Saint Augustine elaborates: "What is Christ saying in these words: *'If you love me, feed my sheep'?* He is saying, 'Do not think to feed yourself, but feed my sheep. Feed them as mine, not as yours. Seek my glory in them, not your own. Seek my lordship, not yours. Seek my gain, not yours.'"

When Saint Paul, as Chrysostom noted, heard these words spoken to Peter, he sought to demonstrate his love for Christ to the highest degree. Indeed, no true minister who genuinely loves God will neglect to feed the flock of God, the sheep of His pasture, who are entrusted to him and rely upon him. On the other hand, the minister who cares only for the fleece, leaving his flock scattered and unattended, reveals his love for the world but shows no true love for God.

PART 6:
God Loved in His Son

Finally, God must be loved in His Son, Jesus Christ, the Son of the Virgin Mary. For Christ declares, *"He that hateth me hateth my Father also,"* (John 15:23), and *"Except ye believe that I am he, ye shall die in your sins,"* (John 8:24). These words highlight the fearful condition of unbelieving Turks, Jews, and pagans.

Christ is supremely worthy of our love. He is the *"chiefest among ten thousand,"* and *"altogether lovely,"* (Song of Solomon 5:10, 16). Being God, He took on our flesh. He came down from heaven that we might ascend to heaven. He became a servant that we might be set free. He became poor to make us rich. He was made a curse so that we might be blessed. He died that we might live. He was crucified so that we might be crowned.

To ensure that our love for Him is true, let us examine it by these two notes.

To love Christ genuinely, two primary evidences are *set forth:*

First, our diligence in knowing and obeying His commandments, even to the point of death. Christ declared, *"If ye love me, keep my commandments,"* (John 14:15). He further stated, *"He that hath my commandments, and keepeth them, he it is that loveth me,"* (John 14:21), and *"He that loveth me not keepeth not my sayings,"* (John 14:24). If we break His commandments at will, prioritizing our gain, games, or other pursuits over His Word, we betray a lack of true love for Him. Genuine love for Christ would make us loath to offend Him, esteeming Him and His commandments above all earthly things.

Secondly, our *effort* to *imitate* Christ demonstrates our love for Him. True love inspires imitation. Christ exemplified mercy, meekness, humility, patience, and zeal for God's glory. He went about doing good, praying for His persecutors: *"Father, forgive them; for they know not what they do,"* (Luke 23:34). Can you, for Christ's sake, pray for your enemies? Can you forgive those who wrong, revile, or hate you? If you can, then you love Christ. But if your heart is proud and unwilling to forgive, where is your love for Him?

Understand this: where Christ is loved, there Christ loves; where Christ loves, there He lives; and where He lives, the flesh and its lusts die. If you live in bitterness, hatred, or revenge, refusing to confront and conquer your sinful passions, Christ does not dwell in you. Without Him, you are in a state of spiritual death, no matter your self-perception. Christ abides only in a heart that is humble, meek, and loving. What ingratitude is shown to Christ when you refuse to pardon those He has pardoned, when you withhold forgiveness from those for whom He died! Consider this: Christ forgave you and gave Himself for you—even you, who had lost yourself through sin. If you cannot forgive for His sake, then surely, you do not love Him.

Let us deal honestly with ourselves. By examining our hearts and actions against these marks of true love, we will discern whether the love of God and His Son, Jesus Christ, truly dwells in us—or whether the love of the world and of self dominates us.

David offers two compelling reasons to love God. The first arises from God's gracious and faithful dealings with those who love and serve Him faithfully. The second stems from His severe justice toward those who, out of pride and stubbornness, reject His rule and refuse to love or serve Him.

The first reason is expressed thus: *"The Lord preserveth the faithful,"* (Psalm 31:23). Faithfulness has a twofold meaning:

1. **Faith in God:** The faithful are those who believe in God and trust His Word. This faith opposes unbelief and doubt, laying hold of God's mercy in Christ for justification.
2. **Integrity and Truthfulness:** A faithful person is one who is just and true in word and deed. To this, treachery, falsehood, and hypocrisy are opposed. As Augustine puts it, *"Faith is doing what you say."* Gregory adds, *"We are truly faithful when we perform in deed what we promise in word."*

In this way, one who truly loves God, keeps His doctrine, and remembers the promises made in baptism—living to fulfill them—is a faithful person. Examples of such faithfulness include:

- **Caleb**, who followed God wholly with a different spirit than the disobedient Israelites and was rewarded with entry into Canaan.
- **Moses**, described as faithful in all God's house.
- **David**, of whom God said, *"I have found David the son of Jesse, a man after mine own heart, which shall fulfill all my will,"* (Acts 13:22).
- **Zacharias and Elizabeth**, who walked blamelessly in God's commandments and ordinances.
- **The martyrs**, who endured torment and death rather than deny Christ or compromise their faith and conscience.

God preserves the faithful. He sometimes delivers them from earthly dangers, as He preserved:

- Noah in the flood,
- Lot from Sodom,
- David from his enemies,
- Daniel in the lions' den,
- The three confessors in the fiery furnace, and,
- Many others, including our own deliverance from the treachery of *the Gunpowder Plot*.

Even more importantly, God preserves the souls of the faithful for eternal joy. He has engraved them on the palms of His hands, and He will never turn away from doing them good. Through His power, He keeps them by faith unto salvation (1 Peter 1:5), ensuring they will receive the end of their faith—the eternal salvation of their souls.

This divine preservation should compel us to love God and remain faithful in our service to Him. The crown of life is promised to the faithful. As we desire others to be faithful to us, let us demonstrate faithfulness to God.

Five Ways to Demonstrate Faithfulness
1. **Knowing and Obeying God's Will:** A faithful servant seeks to know and follow all of the Master's commands. If we refuse to obey in some areas, choosing to follow our own desires, we become hypocrites, like Herod. A faithful servant does not pick and choose obedience but seeks to please in all things.
2. **Remaining Faithful in Adversity:** *"If thou faint in the day of adversity, thy strength is small,"* (Proverbs 24:10). A true friend does not abandon in times of trouble, nor does a faithful Christian deny God or embrace error under persecution. True faith is resilient and unyielding, enduring trials without faltering.

3. **Steadfastness Under Trial:** True faith is like chamomile, which grows stronger when trodden upon. It shines brighter in the darkness, enduring all pressures and challenges without breaking.
4. **Unwavering Loyalty to God's Commandments:** Faithfulness requires adherence to God's law, even when it costs us dearly. A faithful servant prioritizes God's will above personal comfort or worldly gain.
5. **Longing for Greater Union with God:** A heart that is truly faithful to God yearns for deeper fellowship with Him. This longing reflects a love that will not be satisfied until it enjoys the fullness of God's presence in eternity. Like the bride in the Song of Solomon, the faithful soul declares, *"I am sick of love,"* (Song of Solomon 2:5).

Let us strive to demonstrate this faithfulness, loving God with sincerity and serving Him with integrity, until we reach the end of our faith—the salvation of our souls.

Thirdly, a faithful servant takes delight in promoting his master's gain and rejoices in seeing his master's customers increase. Similarly, one who is truly faithful to God finds joy in seeing His kingdom flourish, His Word embraced, His laws obeyed, His graces valued, and His followers multiplied.

Fourthly, consider a master who grants his servant time to manage his own affairs but also sets aside a specific time for the servant to work on his behalf. If the servant not only misuses his own allotted time but also squanders the time meant for his master's service in idleness, gaming, or wickedness, such behavior reveals unfaithfulness. Likewise, those who profane God's holy Sabbath—sanctified for His worship—through commerce, indulgence in pleasures, or other profane activities, demonstrate a lack of faithfulness. Conversely, those who diligently spend their master's designated time in prayer, reading, hearing, meditation, singing psalms, performing acts of mercy, and similar practices reveal themselves as faithful. As they honor His Sabbath on earth, they shall assuredly celebrate an eternal Sabbath in heaven with Him.

Finally, a servant is not deemed faithful merely because he resides in his master's house, wears his livery, eats his food, and listens to him speak. If such a servant fears not to displease his master, corrupts his fellow servants, or secretly conspires with his master's enemies, can he truly be called faithful? Likewise, a man is not proven faithful to God simply because he is admitted to the Church, bears the name of a Christian, or partakes in the sacraments. Baptism and the sacrament itself are of no benefit without sincere faith and obedience. Those who lack fear of God's displeasure, seduce others into sin, and ally themselves with worldly and sinful desires, though they may outwardly appear religious, are unfaithful at heart.

On the contrary, the truly faithful are those who fear God, counsel others towards faithfulness, despise sin, resist Satan, and remain vigilant against spiritual compromise. These demonstrate their faithfulness through unwavering devotion.

In this way, the first reason David provides for loving God is His preservation of the faithful. If we desire His protection, wish to express gratitude for His care, or take delight in His providence, we are bound to love Him. To neglect this duty is to forget ourselves and our own salvation. Without love for Him, we lose our very souls, for only by His presence in our hearts can we truly live.

> *O Love! How shall I describe your greatness? You are mighty and triumphant. You are as strong as death and as unyielding as the grave. Your fiery flames cannot be quenched by waters or drowned by floods. You subdue my understanding for God, bringing my restless ambitions under Christ's rule. You refine my mind as fire purifies metal, enlighten my soul like the sun, sweeten my heart like honey, and gladden me like wine. Without you, I lose everything—my soul, my Savior. But if you dwell in me, though I die to myself, Christ lives in me.*

Part 6: God Loved in His Son

This is the Psalmist's first reason for loving God.

The second reason stems from God's righteous judgment against the proud. These individuals refuse to submit to God or His laws, remaining insolent and abusive toward others better than themselves. David declares, "God rewardeth abundantly the proud doer," signifying that God severely punishes the arrogant for their pride with manifold judgments.

Pride, which is hateful before both God and man, as Syracides states, is a particular vice—a swelling of the heart—whereby individuals count themselves deserving of more honor and dignity than they actually merit. This arises from an overblown opinion of oneself, imagining qualities or virtues one does not possess or exaggerating the measure of those one has.

Pride manifests in two ways: against God and against man.

Against God, pride shows itself in several ways, which I will explain to demonstrate the folly of such arrogance. First, pride is seen when a man imagines himself to be God or desires others to view him as such, as in the case of Caligula, who openly mocked all religion and eventually claimed there was no other god but himself. Second, when men assume that what they have comes from themselves, or if it is granted by God, they believe it is due to their merit. Third, pride manifests when men say in their hearts, "He shall not reign over us," and reject God's ordinances, His Word, Sacraments, ministers, their work, and their authority. Fourth, it is present when someone believes they are perfect, breaking no laws, and capable of performing good deeds that merit eternal life. Fifth, pride occurs when men believe they can do good works by their own strength, saying in their hearts, "We will do this or that—who can stop us?" Sixth, it appears when men disobey God's will under the pretense of humility, as when they argue for praying to saints in heaven, claiming it is a sign of reverence to approach a great King through intermediaries. Yet God says, "Call upon me in the day of trouble," (Psalm 50:15), and Christ echoes, "Come unto me, all ye that labour and are heavy laden, and I will give you rest," (Matthew 11:28). Lastly, pride reveals itself when men murmur against God, expressing anger and dissatisfaction when afflicted by Him.

Pride against man also takes various forms. A proud person envies the success or good fortune of others, as if he alone were deserving of honor. He refuses to acknowledge any superior or equal, as demonstrated by Agamemnon and Pompey, treating his peers as inferiors, his inferiors as servants, and his servants as beasts. His words are boastful, his expressions haughty, and his temper volatile when not praised. Sincere humility is foreign to him; if he appears to relent, it is only to prepare for a more audacious move. If he stoops, it is to leap higher. Unwilling to wait for another to invite him to a higher position, he seeks it by underhanded methods such as bribery, slander, or even poisoning. A low or moderate status is abhorrent to him. When he ascends to a high position, he seeks to prevent others from climbing after him, either pulling up the ladder or restricting access to it.

God opposes such proud and haughty individuals, resisting them and casting them down from their heights. He shakes their lofty positions with whirlwinds, strikes with His lightnings, and punishes them severely and publicly when it pleases Him, as David notes, "abundantly," (Psalm 31:23). The judgments of God upon the proud are numerous and instructive.

The fallen angels, for their pride, were cast out of heaven and remain under God's wrath. When our first parents sought to be like God in their pride, they brought ruin upon themselves and all their descendants. The builders of Babel, in their pride, were scattered, and their language was confused. Haman, in his pride, met his end on the gallows he had prepared for Mordecai. The boastful Goliath was defeated by young David at the height of his arrogance. God warned the proud king of Assyria, Sennacherib, saying, "By the strength of my hand I have done it, and by my wisdom; for I am prudent," (Isaiah 10:13). That very night, God sent His angel to kill 185,000 of Sennacherib's soldiers, and later, his own sons, Adrammelech and Sharezer, murdered him while he worshiped his god Nisroch (2 Kings 19:35-37).

Proud Nebuchadnezzar, for boasting in his power, was driven from human society and made to live as a beast. When he came to his senses, he confessed, "Those that walk in pride he is able to abase," (Daniel 4:37). Holofernes, in his pride, lost his head to Judith, and Antiochus met a similarly gruesome end, his head battered with stones before being severed.

Pharaoh, in his pride against God and His people, suffered numerous plagues and calamities. Timotheus, the Athenian, never succeeded in any endeavor after arrogantly declaring that fortune had no part in his achievements. Apryes, the king of Egypt, who claimed that neither God nor man could remove him from his throne, was strangled. Capaneus, who boasted he would conquer Thebes "whether God willed it or not," was struck by lightning. Ajax, in his arrogance, declared that cowards could win with God's help, but he would achieve glory without Him. He later took his own life with Hector's sword. Herod Agrippa, failing to give glory to God when the people declared, "It is the voice of a god, and not of a man," was struck by an angel and eaten by worms (Acts 12:21-23).

The examples continue: Simon Magus, attempting to fly to heaven by demonic power, was cast down and died from his injuries. Alexander the Great, desiring divine recognition, was later poisoned and perished in Babylon. Empedocles, seeking to prove his divinity, leapt into Mount Etna and was consumed by its flames. Domitian demanded to be worshipped as a god, but he was assassinated by his servants with his wife's consent. His memory was cursed, and his monuments were destroyed.

History records countless judgments of God against the proud. Queen Vanda of Poland, refusing marriage out of arrogance, threw herself into the River Vistula to avoid potential disgrace. In another instance, a Jew in Jerusalem, out of obstinate pride, killed his family and himself rather than accept life and liberty offered by Herod.

God often meets pride with severe punishment, whether through disgrace, affliction, or exposure to sin, to humble the heart and bring repentance. Such was the case with Nebuchadnezzar, who learned humility through his fall, and Peter, who abandoned self-reliance after his denial of Christ. These examples show that God resists the proud but gives grace to the humble.

The consideration of these matters teaches us two important duties: first, to detest, avoid, and completely abandon pride—a vice that is more foolish, degrading, inhumane, and impious than any other.

What could be more foolish than failing to see how frail and fragile all the things of this world are? How quickly they change, and how suddenly and grievously men can lose their riches, glory, greatness, and even life itself? What could be more base and lowly than having one's mind fixed to earthly, fleeting things, failing to consider heavenly and eternal matters? To be puffed up with wealth and honors—transient and vain things that are so prone to change their owners—is both senseless and degrading.

What could be more inhumane and less suited to the dignity of mankind than scorning and despising others, considering everyone else as insignificant compared to oneself? What could be more ungodly than boasting of riches, honors, dignities, noble birth, intelligence, strength, beauty, or virtue as though they were not the free gifts of God, and as though men were not indebted to Him for all these things?

Furthermore, what could be more unjust than pride? A proud man attributes more to himself than he deserves and robs others of the recognition due to them. What could be more contentious than pride? Solomon declares, "Only by pride cometh contention," (Proverbs 13:10). Pride has always been the root of heresies and schisms within the Church and a notorious source of discord in commonwealths, kingdoms, cities, and private households. It is more difficult to maintain peace with the proud than with any other, and it is impossible for two proud people to live in sincere harmony— except, perhaps, in rare cases such as when one person's pride refuses to allow anyone to be above him, and another, proud of his so-called humility, refuses to let anyone be beneath him. In such a scenario, they might manage a semblance of friendship, though both are prideful, albeit in different ways.

Finally, what could be more grotesque and repulsive than the *vice* of pride? It renders a man unlike God, whose likeness is mankind's highest honor, and makes him resemble the devil, the father of pride, who destroyed himself through it. What could be a clearer sign of impending ruin or a more certain cause of destruction than pride? "Pride goeth before destruction, and an haughty spirit before a fall," (Proverbs 16:18). What more hateful and destructive enemy to all virtues and goodness does a man have than pride? Pride robs him of them all. Therefore, just as men take care to avoid thieves who rob and spoil, we must take even greater care to avoid pride, which undermines good works and causes their ruin.

If a humble man becomes proud of his humility, he loses the very humility he claims to possess and becomes puffed up with pride. If a man takes pride in his beauty, he forfeits true beauty and becomes a vain fool. If a man is proud of his wisdom, he turns into a fool; if he boasts of his wit, he becomes as senseless as a donkey. If he is proud of his poverty, he becomes rich only in pride; if he is proud of his riches, he becomes poor in piety. What a terrible and hateful sin pride is! Not only is it evil in itself, but it also corrupts good things, turning them into evil. Just as thunder is said to sour good drink, and as venomous creatures transform whatever they consume into poison, so pride turns all the thoughts, words, and deeds of a proud man into instruments of vanity and self-glorification.

In this way, pride resembles a moth or worm that destroys the very fabric or wood it inhabits. Pride, springing from virtue, corrupts it utterly. There is no good thing so excellent that it does not become tainted and ruined as soon as this vile vice infects it.

It is therefore necessary for us to flee from this wretched vice of pride, which we cannot do unless we humble ourselves before God and His ordinances. We must acknowledge Him as the *free giver* of all good things we possess. We must abandon the mistaken notion that we are better than we truly are. We must seek God for His help, and above all, we must remember that "God resisteth the proud, but giveth grace unto the humble," (James 4:6). As someone has aptly said, pride was born in heaven, but having forgotten the way it fell from there, it can never find the path back again.

The consideration of God's judgments against the proud should also teach us, as David would have us learn, to love the Lord, who hates and abundantly punishes this sin, which ought to be detestable to us as well. Since God stands with us against the proud and, by His hatred of their sin, reveals His goodness, and since He punishes them for being the bitterest enemies of His truest friends, it is fitting for us and all God's saints to delight in Him, love Him, and in that love, submit ourselves to Him.

If we do not love Him, we do not truly love ourselves. But if we love Him sincerely, we love ourselves rightly, and we are not only loved by Him in truth, but also truly beloved of Him. This love from God is of infinitely greater worth than the affection of the entire world apart from Him. We need not concern ourselves with how poorly the world regards us if God is pleased with us. Just as a sober and chaste wife is unconcerned with the opinions of other men so long as her husband esteems and loves her, or as a loyal subject values the affection of their sovereign far more than the approval of all the traitors in the land, so too should we prioritize God's love above all else.

Now may the God of love establish and strengthen this love within our hearts, so that we may live and die in His love. May we, in due time, receive the full and final enjoyment of Him whom we love, and in receiving the reward of our love, may we attain everlasting life and the happiness of our souls. All this is made possible through the merits of His beloved Son, Jesus Christ our Savior. To Him, with the Father and the Holy Ghost—three persons, but one ever-living and ever-loving God—be all love and honor, all praise and power, now and forevermore. Amen.

FINIS

Other Works Published by Puritan Publications

1647 Westminster Confession of Faith 3rd Edition (KJV) Bible

A Biblical Response to Superstition, Will-Worship and the Christmas Holiday by Daniel Cawdrey (1588-1664)

A Devotional on Our Savior's Death and Passion by Charles Herle (1598-1659)

A Discourse on Church Discipline and Reformation by Daniel Cawdrey (1588-1664)

A Glimpse of God's Glory by Thomas Hodges (1600-1672)

A Golden Topaz, or Heart-Jewel, Namely, a Conscience Purified and Pacified by the Blood and Spirit of Christ by Francis Whiddon (d. 1656) 2nd Ed.

A Sermon Against Lukewarmness in Religion by Henry Wilkinson (1566-1647)

A Treatise of the Loves of Christ to His Spouse by Samuel Bolton, D.D. (1606-1654)

Other Works

A Treatise on Divine Contentment by Simeon Ashe (d. 1662)

A Vindication of the Keys of the Kingdom of Heaven into the Hands of the Right Owners by Daniel Cawdrey (1588-1664)

Armilla Catechetica, or a Chain of Theological Principles by John Arrowsmith (1602-1659)

Attending the Lord's Table by Henry Tozer (1602-1650)

Christ Inviting Sinners to Come to Him for Rest by Jeremiah Burroughs (1599-1646)

Christ the Settlement in Unsettled Times – Jeremiah Whitaker (1599–1654)

Ezra's Covenant Renewal and the Pursuit of a Lasting Reformation by Josiah Shute, (1588-1643)

Family Reformation Promoted, and Other Works by Daniel Cawdrey (1588-1664)

God is Our Refuge and Our Strength by George Gipps (n.d.)

Love to God

God Paying Every Man His Due – Francis Woodcock (1614-1649)

God With Us, and Other Works by John Strickland (1601-1670)
God, the Best Acquaintance of Christians by Matthew Newcomen (1610–1669)

God's Voice from His Throne of Glory by John Carter (d. 1655)

Gospel Peace, Or Four Useful Discourses by Jeremiah Burroughs (1599-1646)

Gospel Worship, or, The Right Manner of Sanctifying the name of God in General, in Hearing the Word, Receiving the Lord's Supper, and Prayer by Jeremiah Burroughs (1599-1646)

Gradual Reformation Intolerable by C. Matthew McMahon and Anthony Burgess (1600-1663)

Halting Stigmatized by Arthur Sallaway (b. 1606)

How to Serve God in Private and Public Worship by John Jackson (1600-1648)

Independency A Great Schism by Daniel Cawdrey (1588-1664)

Jacob's Seed and David's Delight by Jeremiah Burroughs (1599-1646)

Jesus Christ God's Shepherd by William Strong (d. 1654)

Making Religion One's Business by Herbert Palmer (1601-1647)

Presumptive Regeneration, or, the Baptismal Regeneration of Elect Infants by Cornelius Burgess (1589-1665)

Primitive Baptism and Therein Infant's and Parent's Rights by Matthew Sylvester (1636–1708)

Puritan Meditations by Francis Rous (1579–1659)

Real Thankfulness by Simeon Ashe (d. 1662)

Reasonable Christianity by Henry Hammond (1605-1660)

Reformation and Desolation by Stephen Marshall (1594–1655)

Love to God

Repentance and Fasting by Peter Du Moulin (1601-1684) and Henry Wilkinson (1566-1647)

Rules for Our Walking With God by Jeremiah Burroughs (1599-1646)

Salvation in a Mystery by John Bond (1612-1676)

Scripture's Self Evidence by Thomas Ford (1598–1674)

Selected Works of Peter Sterry by Peter Sterry (1613–1672)

Sermons From the Halls of Church History: The Writings of A Puritan's Mind Volume 2

Sermons, Prayers, and Pulpit Addresses – Alexander Henderson (1583-1646)

Singing of Psalms the Duty of Christians by Thomas Ford (1598–1674)

Spots of the Godly and of the Wicked by Jeremiah Burroughs (1599-1646)

The All-Seeing Unseen Eye of God and Other Sermons by Matthew Newcomen (1610–1669)

Other Works

The Art of Divine Meditation by Edmund Calamy (1600-1666)

The Art of Happiness by Francis Rous (1579–1659)

The Bible is the Word of God Alone by Adoniram Byfield, (d. 1660) and C. Matthew McMahon

The Certainty of Heavenly and the Uncertainty of Earthly Treasures by William Strong (d. 1654)

The Christian's Duty Towards Reformation by Thomas Ford (1598-1674)

The Church's Need of Jesus Christ by Thomas Valentine (1586-1665)

The Covenant of Life Opened by Samuel Rutherford (1600-1661)

The Covenant of Works and the Covenant of Grace by Edmund Calamy (1600-1666)

The Covenant-Avenging Sword Brandished by John Arrowsmith (1602-1659)

The Difficulties of and Encouragements to a Reformation by Anthony Burgess (1600-1663) and C. Matthew McMahon

The Doctrine of Man's Future Eternity by John Jackson (1600-1648)

The Efficiency of God's Grace in Bringing Gain-Saying Sinners to Christ by Simeon Ashe (d. 1662)

The Eternity and Certainty of Hell's Torments by William Strong (d. 1654)

The Excellency of Holy Courage in Evil Times by Jeremiah Burroughs (1599-1646)
The Excellent Name of God by Jeremiah Burroughs (1599-1646)

The Fall of Adam and Other Works by John Greene (d. 1660)

The Glorious Name of God the Lord of Hosts by Jeremiah Burroughs (1599-1646)

The Glory and Beauty of God's Portion and Other Sermons by Gaspar Hickes, (d. 1677)

The Godly Man's Ark by Edmund Calamy (1600-1666)

Other Works

The Growth and Spreading of Heresy by Thomas Hodges (1600-1672)

The Guard of the Tree of Life, a Discourse on the Sacraments by Samuel Bolton (1606-1654)

The Light of Faith and Way of Holiness by Richard Byfield (1598–1664)

The Manifold Wisdom of God Seen in Covenant Theology by George Walker (1581-1651)

The Nature, Danger and Cure of Temptation by Richard Capel (1586–1656)

The Necessity, Dignity and Duty of Gospel Ministers by Thomas Hodges (1600-1672)

The Precious Seeds of Reformation by Humphrey Hardwicke (n.d.)

The Puritans on Exclusive Psalmody – Edited by C. Matthew McMahon

The Puritans on the Providence of God by Edward Corbet, William Pemble and William Gouge

The Rock of Israel and Other Sermons by Edmund Staunton (1600-1671)

The Saint's Communion With God by William Strong, A.M. (d. 1654)

The Saint's Inheritance and the Worldling's Portion by Jeremiah Burroughs (1599-1646)

The Saint's Will Judge the World, and Other Sermons by Daniel Cawdrey (1588-1664)

The Sermons of William Spurstowe (1605-1666)

The Soul's Porter, or a Treatise on the Fear of God by William Price (1597-1646)
The Spiritual Chemyst, or Divine Meditations on Several Subjects by William Spurstowe (1605-1666)

The Sweetness of Divine Meditation by William Bridge (1600-1670)

The Trial of a Christian's Sincere Love to Christ by William Pinke (1599–1629)

The Wells of Salvation Opened by William Spurstowe (1605-1666)

Other Works

The Worthy Churchman, or the Faithful Minister of Jesus Christ by John Jackson (1600-1648)

The Zealous Christian by Simeon Ashe (d. 1662)

Truth, the Great Business of Our Times by John Maynard (1600-1665)

Zeal for God's House Quickened by Oliver Bowles B.D. (1574-1664?)

Zion's Joy – Jeremiah Burroughs (1599-1646)

www.ingramcontent.com/pod-product-compliance
Lightning Source LLC
Chambersburg PA
CBHW020900160426
43192CB00007B/1006